CW01163611

401 STATISTICS QUESTIONS FOR PSYCHOLOGY STUDENTS

CONNOR WHITELEY

No part of this book may be reproduced in any form or by any electronic or mechanical means. Including information storage, and retrieval systems, without written permission from the author except for the use of brief quotations in a book review.

This book is NOT legal, professional, medical, financial or any type of official advice.

Any questions about the book, rights licensing, or to contact the author, please email connorwhiteley@connorwhiteley.net

Copyright © 2025 CONNOR WHITELEY

All rights reserved.

DEDICATION
Thank you to all my readers without you I couldn't do what I love.

INTRODUCTION

Out of everything you learn as an undergraduate and postgraduate psychology student, I think statistics has to be the only topic the vast majority of students can agree on causes the most anxiety and fear.

Personally, I definitely understand this and I was no stranger to being nervous and anxious about statistics in both my undergrad and postgrad degrees. I just couldn't understand it, I flat out hated R Studio with a burning passion during my Masters and I couldn't understand why we had moved away from SPSS. The statistics software I was taught in my undergraduate.

Yet I overcame a lot of my anxiety and nervousness about statistics. Since if you have a good lecturer, a good textbook and a lot of good resources at your fingertips then you can pass statistics. And you can most definitely thrive.

This book will hopefully be part of you thriving in your statistic classes.

Why Did I Write This Book?

If you're a long-term listener of The Psychology World Podcast then you might be familiar with how much I struggled with statistics throughout my degree. Due to bad teachers, me not understanding some concepts and my struggling with R Studio coding and more.

However, I realised just before my Spring Term exams on my Masters that I have come a long, long way on my psychology journey. Even more so for statistics, because I can understand statistics now and I can pass and thrive in statistic exams.

Therefore, I wanted to show to other psychology students that it is possible, you can learn statistics and you can actually enjoy the process. That is something I never ever thought I would say about statistics.

Overall, I wrote this book for the same two reasons I write all my psychology books. I wanted to help others, which this book thankfully does, and I wanted to show you that you can understand statistics. You don't need to be anxious or nervous.

What Does This Book Cover And Who is This Book For?

Unlike a lot of my other psychology books, this book is written in a very different format because instead of me teaching you and discussing topics as we go along, I use a Question-and-Answer Format.

This might sound a little strange but I wrote this book for undergraduate and postgraduate psychology students, so you could test your knowledge, learn and revise different statistics concepts. Yet as always this book is written in an understandable way as well as the book is laid out in a logical way so the chapters and questions build on each other.

This book isn't meant to be a statistics course in its own right, but it will help your revision, it will help your understanding of statistics and it will help you thrive in your statistic classes.

You'll learn a lot from this book.

Who Am I?

Personally, I always love to know who the author is of the nonfiction I read so I know the information is coming from a good source. In case you're like me, I'm Connor Whiteley GMBPsS, the internationally bestselling author of over 40 psychology books.

In addition, I am the host of *The Psychology World Podcast,* a weekly show exploring a new psychology topic each week and delivering the latest psychology news. Available on all major podcast apps and YouTube.

Finally, I am a psychology graduate studying a Clinical Psychology Masters at the University of Kent, England until September 2025.

So now we know more about each other, let's dive into the great topic of psychology statistics.

401 STATISTICS QUESTIONS FOR PSYCHOLOGY STUDENTS

DATA TYPES, REGRESSION, ANOVA, P-VALUES AND MORE BASICS

Personally, I don't really have a problem making myself look a little foolish from time to time, especially when it comes to the basics of statistics. Since I am a little ashamed to admit that I didn't really learn the different types of data and what exactly they meant until my Masters.

Please don't do that to yourself.

Therefore, the questions in this chapter are what I consider to be the basics of psychology statistics, so these are critical to understand. I would highly recommend you read them, know them off by heart and make sure you can apply this knowledge into practice. You'll have an easier time than I did in statistics for sure.

What Is Nominal Data?

Nominal data is the most basic form of data and this is for labelling variables. For example, types of mental health conditions.

What Is Ordinal Data?
Ordinal data is about order and ranking variables.

What Is Interval Data?
Interval data are numbers without a true 0. Like IQ.

What Descriptive Statistic Is Most Affected By Outliers In Data?
The mean is most affected by outliers.

What Is Positively Skewed Distribution Or Data?
When something is positively skewed, the long tail is longer on the right because it is running up the positive numbers.

What Is Negatively Skewed Distribution Or Data?
When something is negatively skewed, the long tail is longer on the left because it is running down the negative numbers.

What Is A Type 1 Error?
A type 1 error is the rejection of a true null hypothesis.

What is a (alpha) Determined By In Statistics?
a is determined by the researcher.

When are the Differences of The Means most relevant in Psychology Statistics?
The difference of the means is most relevant in an independent groups t-test analysis.

What Are Main Effects In Statistics?
Main effect is the effect of an independent variable on a dependent variable.

When Do You Use A Factorial ANOVA?

You use a factorial ANOVA when you want to look at 2 or more nominal independent variables on an ordinal dependent variable.

What Do Main Effects Look At?

Main effects look at differences amongst marginal effects.

What Do Interactions Look At?

Interactions look at the differences amongst cells that aren't accounted for by the main effects.

What Do Simple Main Effects Look At?

Simple main effects look at one factor within one level of another factor.

What Is The Aim Of Qualitative Research?

Qualitative research aims to explore the meaning participants give to their experiences.

What Is The P-Value In Statistics?

The p-value is the probability you could get a result like the one observed if the null hypothesis was true.

Degrees of Freedom Information

When it comes to degrees of freedom reporting questions, look at how many things are being measured. Like weight and height are two things so it is n-2.

What Is Not An Assumption Of A T-Test?

Groups having different means is NOT an assumption of an independent t-test.

What Does A Null Hypothesis Mean For An ANOVA?

A null hypothesis for an ANOVA is that none of the means are significantly different.

What Tests Can A Bonferroni Test Be Used On?

A Bonferroni test can be run on pairwise pre-planned tests and pre-planned tests only.

What Does Orthogonal Mean In Statistics?

Orthogonal means having variables that can be treated independently.

How Do You Make Contrasts Orthogonal In Psychology Statistics?

For making contrasts orthogonal, you don't have to have equated contrasts nor products of all the alternative conceptional contrasts equal zero.

What is an F Statistic?

An F statistic is the value you get after running an ANOVA or regression analysis. This tells you if the means between the two population are significantly different.

When Is a Two Way ANOVA Used?

A two-way ANOVA is used to analyse data from a study with two independent variables and as many levels as necessary.

What is a Pairwise Analysis?

A pairwise analysis is a comparison between two levels of one IV level and a comparison between two conditions.

How Can You Increase Statistical Power?

You can increase the statistical power by increasing a, increasing the sample size and increasing the difference between the means.

Does Increasing the Variability of The Population Increase Statistical Power?

Increasing the variability of the population does not increase the statistical power of a psychology study.

What Is R-Squared?

In regression, R-squared is a measure of how well the linear regression fits the data. This is given as a percentage from 0% to 100%.

How To Know How Many To Subtract N By In Degrees Of Freedom?

In degrees of freedom, to know whether it is N-1 or N-X (X meaning whatever number). You need to look at how many parameters you have. A parameter is a number that describes a whole number. Therefore, if you're looking at Mean and Standard Deviation then you have two parameters.

What is Central Limit Theorem?

The basic point of Central Limit Theorem is that given enough sample participants even the most skewed data can give you a normal distribution.

What Is A Type 1 Error In Statistics?

A false positive is a type 1 error.

What Is A Type 2 Error In Statistics?

A false negative is a type 2 error.

What Is Alpha In Statistics?

Alpha is the significance or probability of rejecting the null hypothesis when it is true. like a significance of 0.05.

What Is Beta In Statistics?

Beta is the probability of us committing a type 2 error (a false negative).

What Does a (alpha) Test in Statistics?

a (alpha) is the significance level in hypothesis test or acceptable probability of a type 1 error.

What is Standard Deviation?

Standard deviation is the square root of variance.

When is a One-Way ANOVA Used?

A one way ANOVA is used on data with 1 independent variable or factor with as many levels as necessary.

What Type of Test is The Tukey's 'Honesty' Significant Difference test?

The Tukey's 'Honesty' significant difference test is a post-hoc test.

What is a Grand Mean?

A Grand Mean is the average of the means of other cells or subgroups within the dataset.

How Do You Compute a New Variable In SPSS?

In SPSS, to compute a new carriable you need to go to the Transform on the top bar. Then you need to select 'Compute Variable'

What is a t-Statistic?

The t-statistic is used in t-tests to determine where to support or reject the null hypothesis.

How Do You Run Main Effects and Interaction Effects In SPSS?

To run main effects and interaction effects in SPSS, you need to run an ANOVA by going to SPSS analyse, General Linear Model and Univariate. Then you enter your IVs in the fixed factor box and your DV in the DV box.

What Is A Reference Category In Regression?

In a General Linear Model, a reference category is the category all other categories are compared against. This is set up by the user, or it is the category with the highest value.

What Is P-Value Probability?

The p-value probability is you could get the result like the one observed if the null hypothesis was true.

What Are Some Criticisms Of Significance Testing?

4 criticisms of significance testing includes:

- Null hypothesises are almost always false in reality because there are always "some" differences that will show up given enough data. Like drug A and B will never be 100% identical so some differences will be found.

- Small p-value doesn't mean small chance of being wrong because in 1 review 74% of studies with a small p-value were wrong. (Granted I got this criticism from a source in the early 2000s so this probably has a temporal validity issue).

- Statistical error is only 1 small part of real error.
- Statistical significance is not the same as scientific significance. Science deals with questions of effect size, not whether an effect exists.

What Is The Error Testing Approach To Significance Testing Called?

The error testing approach to significance testing is called Neyman-Pearson

What Can Influence Effect Size?

Mean difference, methodology and variability can all influence effect size but sample size does not.

What is Multiple R?

Multiple R is the correlation between X and Y.

What is Multiple R-Squared?

Multiple R-squared is the proportion of variance in Y that is accounted by the regression equation.

What Are b And beta Coefficients?

The b and beta coefficients are used in regression to measure the relationship between the dependent and one or more independent variables. b is used to represent one unit change in an independent variable. Whereas beta coefficients represent 1 change in standard deviation for the independent variables.

What Is Least Square Criterion?

The Least Square Criterion is a test used to test the accuracy of a straight line in depicting the data it was made from.

What Is Statistical Power?

Statistical power is the probability that a test will detect an effect or difference in data when it exists.

What Is A Power Analysis Made Up Of?

A power analysis is made up of the effect size, the power, the significance level and the sample size and one of its components.

What Can Power Analysis Be Used For?

You can use a power analysis for:

- Comparing different statistical tests and choosing the test with the highest power to detect an effect of interest.
- Calculating the optimal sample size for a given sample effect size and significance level, and vice versa.
- Calculating the minimum sample size needed to achieve a certain level of statistical power and significance level.

What Is The Recommended Effect Size In Psychology Statistics?

80% is the generally recommended effect size in psychology.

What Do Sensitivity Tests Measure?

Sensitivity tests measure how well a test can identify a presence or absence of a particular outcome or condition.

What Do One-Way ANOVAs Analyse?

A one-way ANOVA analyse the difference between two or more groups.

What Data Does A Chi-Square Test Use?

A chi-square test uses categorical data.

What are F-Ratios?

The f-ratio measures the variance between group means and compares it to the variance within groups. Higher f-ratio values mean there are greater differences whereas lower f-ratio values mean there are lower or no differences.

What are F-Tests?

An F-test compares the variances of 2 or more groups of data based on F-ratio. F-tests can be used for testing the good fit of a regression model, testing the difference between 2 or more means in an ANVOA, or testing the equality of variances.

What Is A Sum Of Squares Error?

A sum of squares error is a calculation that measures the difference between predicted and actual values. It's used to evaluate the accuracy of a regression model where a lower SSE shows the model is a better fit for the data.

What Are Type 1 Sum Of Squares?

Type 1 sum of squares is where all the variances of the main effects is given to the first main effect entered.

What Are Type 3 Sum Of Squares?

Type 3 sum of squares is where all the shared variance amongst the main effects and interactions is discarded, so all the main effects and interaction control for each day.

What Are Type 2 Sum Of Squares?

Type 2 sum of squares gets rid of the shared variance of the main effects, but not the shared variance between the main effects and interactions.

BASIC R STUDIO QUESTIONS

At the end of each chapter from this point onwards, there will be some questions and answers about how to compute or use these topics in data analysis if you use R Studio. Personally, I wanted to include these basic questions because rather silly of me, I didn't learn the basics of R Studio until later on. If I had learnt R Studio earlier then I could have saved myself a lot of confusion and a lot of stress.

What Is A Vector In R Studio?

In R Studio, a vector is a series of data points of the same basic type. For example, participant scores.

What Is A List In R Studio?

A list is an ordered collection of elements of different types. Like, functioning vectors and more.

What Is A Factor In R Studio?

A factor in R Studio stores nominal values as a vector integers (whole numbers) in the specific range as well as an internal vector of character strings mapped to these integers.

What Is A Data Frame In R Studio?

A Data Frame is a two-dimensional structure or table consisting of variables (vectors) organised into columns. These can be made-up of different data types unlike a matrix.

What Is A Matrix In R Studio?

A matrix is a two-dimensional rectangular data structure consisting of values of the same basic type. For example, numerical data. Also, you can use a matrix by joining together numbers of vectors of the same length and type together, and these can be created by combining vectors.

How Do You Get Rid of Objects From The Environment In R Studio?

You need to use the rm() function and inside the brackets you put the name of the object you want to get rid of.

What Function Is Used To Create Factors?

In R Studio use the factor(x, levels, labels=levels) to encode a vector as a factor. For instance, sex<-factor(sex, levels=C(1,2), labels=C("male", "female"))

How Do You Create a Basic Scatter Plot In R?

You use the plot(x, y) function to create a scatter plot where you need to specific what x and y actually are. Such as *plot(data name$variable1, data name$variable 2)*

What Is Another Name For The psych Package?

Sometimes the psych package is called the GP Arotation package.

How Do You Reverse Code Items In R Studio?

You need to use the reverse.code() function using 1 or -1 on each item to tell R what items are and are not reverse coded. If you have five items and only the fourth item is -1, then you are telling R that only the fourth item is reserve coded. For example, R_conduct <- reverse.code(c(1,-1,1,1,1), SDQ[items_conduct]).

PSYCHOMETRICS AND PSYCHOLOGICAL MEASURES

I think this is a great chapter to kick-off the deep-dive sections of the book because psychometrics and psychological measurements, are essentially the lifeblood of psychology as a science. Due to if we didn't use psychometrics and if we didn't have valid, reliable measures then psychology wouldn't be a science and that would be awful.

Then again, this is an issue that no one normally thinks about, because I never think about psychometrics and measurements. And that's slightly concerning because in clinical psychology we want to measure and track someone's mental health condition with accuracy and reliability.

I'm hardly alone.

I don't think I know too many applied or even theoretical psychologists who focus on psychometrics and psychological measurements. Leading us to use the same tools and scales over and over again without anyone truly focusing on how good they actually are.

This is the focus and aim of the various topics that we're going to be looking at in this book.

What Is A Measurement?

In statistics, a measurement is the assignment of numbers to a quantifiable attribute according to a rule. Also, this rule can be arbitrary so this allows for multiple assignments. For example, temperature can be measured in Fahrenheit or Celsius, which are two different scales/ assignments. As well as these two scales can be turned into each other because they have a linear transformation.

Equally, this assignment can be non-linear because the Richter scale is a way to measure earthquakes. Each number means the earthquake is 10 times more powerful than the previous number. Therefore, if an earthquake has a value of 10 on the Richter scale then it is 10 times more powerful than an earthquake that has a value of 9.

What Is Scaling?

In statistics, scaling is the process of setting up the rule of correspondence between observations and numbers assigned. As well as McDonald (1999) added that data and observations are very different, because data are scaled observations.

What Are Noisy Measurements?

According to Henk Kelderman noisy measurements are outcomes that are considered indicators of a given attribute but these indicators cannot be directly observed.

What Are Some Examples of Noisy Observations?

Noisy observations can include non-response, recall, subjectivity, response styles and self-deception as well as motivated misresponse.

What Are Psychometrics?

In psychology statistics, psychometrics focuses on the development of formal methods and theories that help us to study the fidelity and appropriateness of different psychological measurements.

In addition, Dr Henk Kelderman writes at http://www.psychometrika.org/society/index.html):

"Measurement and quantification is ubiquitous in modern society. In early modernity, the scientific revolution provided a firm scientific basis for physical measures like temperature, pressure, and so on. In the late nineteenth and early twentieth century, a similar revolution took place in psychology with the measurement of intelligence and personality. A crucial role was played by Psychometrics, initially defined as "The art of imposing measurement and number upon operations of the mind."

Since 1936 the Psychometric Society has been at the forefront of the development of formal theories and methods to study the appropriateness and fidelity of psychological measurements. Because measurement in psychology is often done with tests and questionnaires, it is rather imprecise and subject to error. Consequently, statistics plays a major role in psychometrics. For example, members of the society have devoted much attention to the development of statistical methods for the appraisal of noisy measurements whose outcomes are considered indicators of attributes of interest that cannot be directly observed.

Today, psychometrics covers virtually all statistical methods that are useful for the behavioral and social sciences including the handling of missing data, the combination of prior information with measured data, measurement obtained from special experiments, visualization of statistical outcomes, measurement that guarantees personal privacy, and so on. Psychometric models and methods now have a wide range of applicability in various disciplines such as education, industrial and organizational psychology, behavioral genetics, neuropsychology, clinical psychology, medicine, and even chemistry."

What Are Some Ways To Collect Observations In Psychology?

To gather observations you could collect reaction times, self-reports, peer ratings, time to relapse, time in remission, basal level of skin conductance and many, many more.

What Is Theory of Data?

According to Coombs (1960), his Theory of Data classifies the essential focus of every psychological measurement we use in the discipline is to associate each construct of interest, stimulus or individual to a point in a psychological space. Also, he mentioned in his 1960 paper that "basically, all a person can do is to compare stimuli with each other, or against some absolute standard or personal reference point."

How Many Categories Are Optimal For Likert Scaling?

Whilst it is technically true that more categories mean more data points, in reality, 5 categories are optimal in Likert Scaling. Since research shows participants cannot meaningfully differentiate between more than 7 categories.

What Is Another Name For Optimal Scaling?

Correspondence analysis is another name for optimal scaling.

What Is Optimal Scaling?

This type of scaling derives its values for response options that are statistically optimal. For example, Optimal Scaling seeks to maximise the internal consistency of a scale (also known as the correlations between the stimuli measuring the same thing).

How Are Test Scores Assigned?

A test score in statistics is assigned using one of the scaling methods. As well as test score is the weighted sum of the item scores or it is the sum of the items scores. The weight of each item score is determined before scoring as well as optimal scaling and judgemental scaling assign their weights to basic responses.

What Is A Criterion-Referenced Measurement?

This is a measurement that is referenced by a pre-defined standard of behaviour (this is the criterion). Since the criterion is the area of a subject that the test is designed to measure. For example, a criterion for a diagnosis of social anxiety disorder might be a client must endorse 80% of items on a questionnaire. This is a criterion-referenced measurement because you don't need to compare this client to anyone else, you only been to reference their scores to criterion.

What Is A Norm-Referenced Measurement?

This is when a measurement is based on the distribution of scores obtained from the population that the researchers interested in. This is basically the "norm" that everyone is compared against.

What Is Thurstone's Law of Comparative Judgement?

His Law of Comparative Judgement from 1927 proposes that each stimulus must elicit a psychological value from a participant. As well as the respondents should choose the stimulus with the highest psychological value at the moment of comparison with these values being distributed normally in the population.

What Is An Example of Measurement By Fiat?

Likert scaling is an example of measurement by Fiat because researchers have arbitrarily decided how to assign numbers to a response so this assignment lacks any empirical justification.

What Are Some Examples of Measurement of Modelling?

Since measurement by modelling involves scores that are based on models for stimulus respondent behaviour, Guttman and Thurstonian scaling are good examples.

What Is Type 1 Data In Psychology Statistics?

Type 1 data or Type 1 Observations are preferential choices where the participant is asked which of the two stimuli they prefer.

What is Type 2 Data?

Type 2 data is Single Stimulus where participants are asked where they stand in relation to the stimulus.

What is Type 3 Data?

Type 3 Data is stimulus comparison where participants are asked which of the two stimuli have more of some attributes.

What Is Type 4 Data?

Type 4 Data is Similarities where participants are asked which of the two pairs of stimuli are more alike.

What Type of Data Is Used In Multidimensional Scaling?

Similarities (Type 4 Data) is used in Multidimensional scaling.

What Type Of Data Does Thurstonian Scaling Use?

Thurstonian Scaling works for both Type 1 Data (preferential choice) and stimulus comparison (Type 3 Data).

What Is Thurstonian Scaling?

In 1927, Thurstone proposed a way to estimate population means of stimuli from their rank orderings in a sample drawn from the population of interest. Therefore, all means can be estimated in relation to the mean of some "referent" stimulus if we follow some basic rules of comparative judgements which he called Thurstone's Law of Comparative Judgements.

What Does The names() function do in R Studio?

The names() function allows you to quickly see the variable names in a dataset.

What Does The head() function do?

In R Studio, the head() function shows you the first few rows of a dataset. This is normally the first 6 rows because this is the default on R.

What Does The tail() function do?

Unlike the head() function, the tail () shows you the last few rows of a dataset.

What Does The describe() function print?

By using the describe() function, you can get the descriptive statistics, like mean, range, median, number and more for your dataset.

What Is The lowerCor() function?

This function allows a researcher to compute the product-moment (Pearson) Correlations between items.

Why Would You Use lowerCor() from the Psych package over Cor() in Base R for a reliability analysis?

The lowerCor() function is better for reliability analysis because this function only shows you the lower triangle of a correlation matrix. This is more compact and it's easier to read and understand than the cor() function.

What Is tetrachoric() function used for?

In R Studio, you use the tetrachoric() for calculating the tetrachoric correlations within a dataset.

How Can You Estimate Cronback's alpha (Internal Consistency Reliability) in R Studio?

You can use the alpha() function in R from the psych package to estimate Cronbach's alpha.

What Is The Formula For Computing Standard Error of Measurement for Total Score?

You can use this formulation to compute the Standard Error of Measurement using the tetrachorics-based alpha, $SEm(y) = SD(y)*sqrt(1-alpha)$. You're going to need the standard deviation value for the total score.

What Function Do You Use In R Studio To Create Variable Lists?

You can use the c() function to create variable lists and then you list the variables inside. For example, if you wanted to create a list of variables called *Emotions* then you would do the following: *Emotions <- c("happy", "sad", "scared", "rage")* or whatever your dataframe requires.

What Function Could You Use To Compute Test Scores In R Studio?

Once you have your variable lists, you can use the rowSums() function to calculate the sum of specific variables for each respondent. For instance, rowSums(dataframe name [Emotion]).

Using the rowSums() function, how do you get rid of NA responses?

To get rid of any NA responses with the rowSums() function, you need to add "na.rm=TRUE" to the end of the code. Such as *rowSums(dataframe name [Emotion], na.rm=TRUE).*

For Norm Referencing In R Studio, How Do You See How Many Participants Are Within A Normal Range For A Measure?

Firstly, you need to check your measure to see what is defined as normal. For example, if an emotional measure says scores less than 5 are within normal range then you need to tell R Studio to tell you how many participants have scores under 5.

To do this, you need to create a table in R Studio that gives you the information you want.

When it comes to cut-offs, you want to use this code *table(dataframe name$variable name <- cutoff)* and an example of this is *table(Data$Emotion<-5)*.

Then R Studio will give you a table with FALSE or TRUE with numbers underneath. In this case, you're interested in the number under TRUE because this is the number of respondent with a number under your cutoff, so these are within normal range.

Equally, if a person needs a cut-off of over a set number then you simply switch the maths symbol so it becomes "greater than". For example, *table(Data$Emotion>-5)*.

CLASSICAL TEST THEORY

As we continue to explore different aspects of psychological measurements and the statistical basis of psychology as a science, we're now going to be looking at questions around items and Classical Test Theory.

As much as I never want to admit this, it was this topic that made me start thinking about doing some kind of psychology statistics book. Since this is a very interesting, useful and thought-provoking topic. As well as I was creating a second study when I was learning this so it was really useful to understand this content.

It's still a topic I regularly draw on even now.

<u>What Are The Two Types of Test Items?</u>

Item scores in statistics can be binary or Quantitative test items.

<u>What Are Binary Test Items?</u>

Binary test items are dichotomous and two-valued test items that can be developed from different responses formats. For example, yes or no answers, multiple choice questions amongst others.

In addition, a keyed response like "pass" is often coded as 1 whereas an unkeyed response like "fail" is often coded 0.

What Are Quantitative Test Items?

On the other hand, Quantitative test items can result from different response formats, like judgemental or Likert scaling. Also, it's important to note that you should almost never take a sufficiently wide range of values to mean anything more than ordered categories. Yet we can often assume them to be interval variables.

What Is The Item Mean For Binary Items?

When it comes to binary items, the item mean is the proportion of passes or "keyed responses".

How Would You Define Item Difficulty For Binary Test Items?

When it comes to binary test items, the difficulty is the probability that a respondent will pass the item. In terms of non-cognitive tests, it's easier to think of passing as giving the keyed response to the item. Whereas for cognitive test items, it's easier to think about binary test item difficulty as if an item is too easy then this is an item that everyone passes. Or if everyone fails an item then it is too difficult.

What Is The Mean For Quantitative Test Items?

The mean of Quantitative test items is related to item difficulty because we can think of non-quantitative items as "difficulty to endorse". Therefore, items with a low mean are difficult to endorse whereas items with high means are easy to endorse. An example of a non-quantitative item would be responding to a statement on a 5-point Likert Scale like "I Believe Everyone Gets What They Deserve In Life".

What Is The Ceiling Effect?

The ceiling effect is when everyone passes the test item because it is an easy item.

What Is The Floor Effect?

The floor effect is a test item that has high difficulty so everyone fails it.

Why Are The Ceiling and Floor Effects A Problem?

Whilst it is true that we need easy items to differentiate between people that have low levels of the attribute we're researching, we also can't only have difficult items because people at the below average level of the attribute won't pass any of these difficult items. Therefore, this is a massive problem for researchers because we won't to be to see any individual differences in that group because everyone would end up with the same score.

In addition, if we had some easy items and some items that were more difficult, some people would pass them and this would allow us to differentiate between people.

How Is Variance Calculated In Binary Test Items?

The variance in a binary test item is calculated by the mean because of an equation that is too complicated to write out in this book. Yet the variance equals the average of all squared values of the variable we're looking at minus the squared mean.

Therefore, when it comes to binary test items, the possible values of X is only 0 or 1 (because there are only two values for binary items). This means that the sum of squared values will be equal to the number of values that were equal to 1 (in other words the number of people that passed the item). Afterwards we divide that number by the item mean to give us our variance.

How is Variance Calculated In Quantitative Item Statistics?

Even though Quantitative items only have a limited number of responses, the variance is still determined by the mean because there are limits on the minimum and maximum possible scores. Since it isn't possible to have the mean move forward to such an extreme value without the variance becoming smaller, and as McDonald (1999) said "diversity prevents an average extreme view".

Why Isn't Pearson Correlation Effective For Binary Items?

For binary items looking at continuous variables, they will never have two means or difficulties that are exactly the same so even though they might be perfectly correlated, they have different means. For instance, Celsius and Fahrenheit. Therefore, binary items that have different difficulties can never be perfectly associated when Pearson Correlation is used.

This is why Pearson Correlation is plausible to use for binary items that have the exact same means because the result will show they are perfectly correlated. This perfect correlation of 1 just isn't possible for continuous variables when Pearson Correlation is used.

Are Binary items Truly Dichotomies?

No, most binary items are not true dichotomies because they're "Quantitative response tendencies" that have been dichotomised. As a result, the observed response of X is the dichotomised response tendency of X as well as if we assume X is normally distributed then the threshold can be found from observed proportions and normal distribution tables.

What Is Tetrachoric Correlation?

The Tetrachoric Correlation is the Pearson correlation of two normal (underlying) response tendencies. Also, this is estimated from 2x2 cross-tabulations or the raw data itself by the threshold first being estimated before the correlation is estimated. Then any further data analysis that you want to do you have to continue doing with the tetrachoric correlations.

How Does Correlation Work For Quantitative Item Statistics?

When it comes to Quantitative items, if these are examples of interval data then we can use product-moment correlations. As well as when there are only a few categories being used then the product-moment correlation tends to underestimate the correlation between underlying response tendencies.

On the whole, the polychoric correlation is the linear correlation of the two underlying normal response tendencies that were categories. And thankfully this is easy to calculate in R Studio.

What Is The True-Score Model For Test Scores?

This reliability theory argues that an observed test score is the sum of the true score that we cannot score and the random error of our measurement. This is another aspect we cannot directly observe.

Also, there are three assumptions that this model relies on.

What Are The Assumptions Of The True-Score Model?

Firstly, the model assumes that the test score error is not correlated with the true score, so the error score doesn't depend on the level of ability or whatever variable you want to measure in your research.

Secondly, we're assuming that the error score might go up or down across a lot of test administrations, and yet error score will still be normally distributed with the expected mean score of 0.

Finally, we assume that for any two independent measurements of the variable of interest, their error scores are uncorrected. So we end up assuming error has a truly random influence on the test score.

What Is The Standard Error of Measurement?

The Standard Error of measurement is the standard deviation of error in the normal distribution. This is a critical aspect of classical test theory because we need to know Standard Error of measurement so we can understand the expected spread of observed scores. In other words, this allows us to estimate an interval where the observed score will fall in the given percentage of repeated test administration for the same respondent.

Also, a small Standard Error of measurement will give you higher confidence about the location of the true score.

What Is Score Reliability?

Score reliability is the proportion of variance because of the true score is the reliability of test score. As well as the reliability is bound between 0 and 1 and the variance between the True and Error component is partitioned, because they're uncorrelated.

What Does A Reliability of 0 and 1 mean for Score Reliability?

If a score has a reliability of 0 then this means all the variance for that item score is down to random error. Whereas a reliability of 1 means all the variance is due to the true score, so as you can guess most of the measures within psychology falls somewhere in-between.

How Do You Estimate Reliability?

As a result of us not knowing the True score variance, we need to use four different methods of estimating the reliability, and researchers typically only use one of these methods.

Firstly, we can use test-retest as long as it meets the three conditions. The True score doesn't change between administrations, the errors of the two measurements are uncorrelated, as well as test measures that have equal precision are used on both occasions. This helps us to estimate reliability because the proportion of variance because of the true score equals the correlation between Test and Retest Scores. This helps to make it very easy to estimate reliability using this method.

Secondly, we can create two forms (parallel forms) of the test as long as the two forms measure the same attribute with equal precision and the errors of each form are uncorrelated. Therefore, the proportion of variance because of the true score again equals the correlation between the scores on both forms of the test. Therefore, it's easy to estimate score reliability with parrel forms.

We'll look at the third and fourth methods in another question.

What Is The Problem With The Test-Retest Method?

Firstly, the problem with the test-retest method is that it generally underestimates the reliability because any changes in the True score will be seen as "error" and the condition assumes participants don't pick up any practice effects, memory factors or fatigue in the time between the two tests being administered. Which just isn't realistic in the real world.

Secondly, the test-rest correlation is influenced by the stability of the variable or attribute over time as well as the precision with which the test measures the True score. Since you just cannot separate these influences from only two measurements.

What Are The Problems With The Parallel Form Method?

The main problem with the parallel form method is that the correlation is influenced by the very extent to which the two forms are actually parallel. Since the extent to which the two forms actually measure the same attribute can be different, as can the precision by which the two forms measure it.

In addition, the alternate forms correlation can give you an imprecise estimate of the reliability because of the lack of parallelism.

On the whole, whilst parallel forms reliability can be a very good way to estimate test precision, it is really challenging because creating truly parallel forms aren't easy.

What Is The Split-Half Method?

To avoid wasting resources by asking participants to come in twice for the same test or wasting our own time creating another test, we can use the Split-Half method to get two scores for each person. Since we can get two subtests by splitting the test in two halves and treating them as two subtests. Of course, we have to make sure the two halves measure the same attribute with equal precision and the error of each half are uncorrelated.

This allows us to estimate the reliability because the proportion of variance because of the true score on either subtest is equal to the correlation between the scores on the first and second subtest. Therefore, this allows us to easily estimate the reliability.

Nonetheless, the challenge with the spilt-half method is to not only create a fair split, but to project what the reliability of the whole test would be if we know the reliability of its halves.

This is where Spearman-brown Prophecy Formula comes in.

What Is The Spearman-Brown Prophecy Formula?

The Spearman-Brown prophecy formula is a formula that predicts the reliability of the score on a shorter or longer test made up of items from the given test. With the reliability of the given test score being denoted by "rho 1" in the formula and this is the test we start with.

Then if you increase the length of the test n times then the reliability will be greater as well as if we reduce the length of the test and times, the reliability will be smaller.

This gives us a test's projected reliability.

What's The Problem With Split-Half Estimation?

As a result of there being a lot of different ways to split a test in half, like divide it straight down the middle, do odd and even items or a random split. All these different splits with give you a different estimate for your test reliability.

Also, if you use the odd item/ even item split and you don't have the same number of items in each half then you need to make corrections.

What Is Internal Consistency as a Measurement of Score Reliability?

This method treats each item of a test as an independent measure if the items all measure the same attribute, all items contribute equally to the measurement of T (true-score equivalent items) and the errors of all these items are uncorrelated.

What Is the Coefficient "alpha" in terms of score reliability?

The coefficient "alpha" estimates score reliability from test items with Louis Guttman in 1945 generalising all computational forms of alpha and he showed that alpha is the mean of spilt-half coefficients resulting from all different splits of a test.

Why Might You Use The corr.test() function for factor analysis?

You might want to use the corr.test() function in R Studio because this allows you to check the correlations between responses in items. So this function prints pairwise sample sizes, corresponding p-values and full correlation matrix. Equally, you could just use the lowerCor() function to only get the correlation matrix.

What Does The KMO() function do In R Studio?

In R Studio, the KMO() function is useful for getting the Kaiser-Meyer-Olkin Index. This is a measure of sampling adequacy (MSA). An example of some code using this function would be KMO(SDQ[items_conduct]).

What Does The fa.parallel() function do?

This function helps us to create Parallel Analysis Scree plots so we know how many factors to retain in our analysis.

What Function Do You Use To Run A Factor Analysis?

In R Studio, you use the fa() function to a factor analysis for a single-factor model. This is why you need to tell the function how many factors you're using, from the number of factors you're retaining from your scree plot. An example of this code in action is fa(SDQ[items_conduct],nfactors=1).

After running a factor analysis in R Studio, how do you get a more detailed output of the residuals?

To get a more detailed output of the residuals, you need to use the fa() function again but this time, you need to create a new object so you can run more analyses on it later. For example, F_conduct <- fa(SDQ[items_conduct], nfactors=1).

What R Studio Function Do You Use To Get Residuals From The Saved Factor Analysis Results?

The residuals.psych() function is a useful function to get residuals from saved objects and your results are printed in a user-friendly way too.

Why Do You Need To specify Number of Factors With The omega() function?

Since the omega() function is designed for multi-factor models, you should always specify the number of factors of the model you have in the code. Even more so for single-factor models. An example of the code in practice would be *omega(R_Emotion, nfactors=1)*.

TEST HOMOGENEITY AND TEST VALIDITY

When it came to writing this book and designing where to put the different questions so you can learn and understand as much as possible, I needed to create an order that allowed content to build on each other.

Thankfully, this worked with 99% of the chapters but this one was a little more difficult. Since this topic deals with test validity, homogeneity and it dips into factor analysis too. Therefore, it was a little difficulty knowing to stop and start the questions because at this point I was writing the questions without dividing them up into topics. Silly me.

I was glad I was able to save this chapter and make it useful, interesting and packed with questions that will benefit your revision and learning for sure.

What Is A Homogeneous Test?

Whilst this is sometimes called a unidimensional test, a homogeneous test is a test with items that only measure one attribute in common.

Why Must Items In A Homogenous Test Correlate With Each Other?

The items need to correlate with each other in a homogenous test because they all measure the same psychological attribute. Yet it is important to note that there should only be a single cause of this correlation to make sure the items are only measuring one common attribute. If there are more than one common cause then this test isn't valid for the attribute as it isn't homogeneous.

What Is A Common Factor?

A common factor is the term given for the common cause that makes all the items in a homogeneous test correlate with each other.

What Are The Origins Of Factor Analysis?

In an effort to find a common factor that explained the similarity of scores on all intelligence tests, Spearman wanted to describe the relationship between test scores on a wide range of domains. For example, intelligence on English, French, Mathematics, Classics amongst others. Therefore, in his 1904 paper, he proposed the idea of a "general intelligence" factor (g) to provide a way to explain the correlation between these variables.

Also, it's worth noting the words of Jenson (1998):

"Virtually all present day researchers in psychometrics now accept as a well established fact that individual differences in all complex mental tests are positively correlated, and that a hierarchical factor model, consisting of a number of group factors dominated by g at the apex (or highest level of generality), is the best representation of the correlational structure of mental abilities."

What Is Reliability?

In statistics, reliability is concerned with the extent to which the test score can be reproduced. It couldn't care less about the validity of a measure.

What Is Validity?

According to McDonald (1999), validity is the "extent to which a test measures the attribute it is used to measure". In other words, if you want to measure depression, then your test actually needs to measure depression for it to be valid, but if it measured anxiety instead then it would be invalid.

What Is Evidence Of Validity?

Referring to McDonald (1999), "Confirmation that the test is psychometrically homogeneous together with a convincing conceptual analysis jointly constitutes evidence of validity."

Then you can test the homogeneity of a scale by confirming that a factor model fits the data as well as you need to do a conceptual analysis to confirm that the correct attribute is being measured by the scale you're using.

What Is A Single-Factor Model?

A single-factor model is a set of items where every item can be presented as a linear combination of the common factor that the researcher wants to focus on, and each item is made up of a "unique" part too. This unique part can be called error as well. As well as the unique part of each item is independent from the common factor and they are independent from each other, with this being called "local independence" at times.

How Is Factor Score Scaled?

Since Factor Score isn't observed, it doesn't have any natural scale so in statistics, we typically set the scale as if Factor Score is a standardised variable so the mean(F0=0 and var(F)=1.

What Is Item Factor Loading?

Item Factor Loading reflects how sensitive the item is to changes in the factor score, as well as on graphs this is represented by the slope.

What Is Item Mean On A Graph?

The Item mean is the intercept on a graph and this reflects the typical response of a respondent with a factor score of 0.

What Is Factor Analysis?

Factor Analysis is the process of fitting a common factor model to a dataset, and factor analysis allows us to find a small set of factors that explains the covariation in a larger set of observed variables. Also known as test items.

Why Can Item Variance Be Partitioned?

We can partition item variance because the variance is made up of the common factor and unique variance. In essence, there are two sources of variances so we can partition them out.

How Is "Fitting" Done In Factor Analysis?

To test the fit of a model to a dataset, computer algorithms search for parameter values that make represent the observed variables throughout a single-factor model. This is mainly done by using two common methods: the method using minimising residuals and maximum likelihood.

What Is The Maximum Likelihood Method of Fitting?

This method of "fitting" works by maximising the probability (likelihood) of the sample observations so it assumes you have large samples and normal data to help it find the parameter values.

What Is The Minimising Residuals Method of Fitting?

This method of "fitting" involves minimising the residuals (these are the squared differences between the observed and reproduced correlations) and it uses unweighted least squares and it works well for non-normal data and small samples.

How Is The Hypothesis of The Factor Model Holds The Population Tested?

Computer software compares the probability of the sample data if the hypothesis of homogeneity is true to the probability of the data if the observations could have come from a population without any restrictions (this is known as the unrestricted covariance matrix). Also, the difference in probabilities is showed as a chi-square output with the degrees of freedom equal to the number of known variances and covariances minus the number of parameters to estimate.

Furthermore, researchers hope to retain this hypothesis instead of rejecting it so they want a p-value greater than 0.05.

What is The Measure of Sampling Adequacy?

In 1970, Kaiser proposed the Measure of Sampling Adequacy (MSA) to see if a factor model is likely to be appropriate for a dataset. The MSA relates the size of the variable inter-correlations to the pairwise partial correlations that account for all the other variables in the given dataset.

Furthermore, if the correlations are all around 0 then as you would expect the MSA tends to be 0. Also, when there is no common factor and the partial correlations are the same as the pairwise correlations, the MSA tends to be 0.5. Then if there is a common factor and the partial correlations around 0 then MSA tends to be 1.

What Are The MSA Guidelines?

According to Kaiser, here are the following guidelines that should help you understand how to use MSA. If you have a MSA score of 0.0 to 0.5 then a factor model is going to be "totally useless" whereas if you have a score of 0.5-0.6 then the factor model will have "miserable" usefulness. And I promise these labels are actually what Kaiser wrote down.

In addition, if you have a MSA of 0.6-0.7 then the factor model will have mediocre use, a MSA of 0.7-0.8 will have middling usefulness and a MSA of 0.8-0.9 means you'll have meritorious data for a factor model. As well as if you have a MSA score between 0.9 and 1 then have marvellous data for a factor model.

How Can You Use A Scree Test To See How Many Factors You Have?

If you only need one factor to describe a dataset then this one factor must explain most of the variance in the variance-covariance matrix. Then if you remove this variance (controlling for the factor itself), then the items that made up this homogeneous set must only have the variances that are caused by its unique parts left over. Then as a result of these parts being unique so they don't correlate, if we tried to extract another factor then this shouldn't be possible. Since this second factor should explain very little about the residual variance-covariance matrix.

This was an idea proposed by Raymond Catell in 1966.

Therefore, the scree plot shows you the variance associated with the first factor, second factor and so on. When it comes to homogenous items, it's the first variance that accounts for the most amount of variance then there should be a sharp drop in the amount of variance explained by each later factor.

To interpret a scree plot, you look at the number of factors above the "elbow" and that is the number of factors you have in your dataset.

What Is Parallel Analysis?

Parallel Analysis is the objective method that is based on the scree plot because it compares the observed scree plot with a scree plot for a simulated random (uncorrelated) dataset of the same size so the analysis uses it as a baseline comparison.

What Is Alpha In Terms of Reliability?

Alpha gives us a good estimate of the reliability of a test when this test is made up of homogeneous items with approximately equal factor loadings.

How Is Alpha Abused?

About 95% of the psychology literature abuses alpha because that 95% argues alpha uses evidence for test homogeneity when it doesn't. This is why you should assess the homogeneity of a test before you compute alpha.

What is Omega?

Omega is the coefficient of the reliability of a sum score that applies to all homogeneous tests. Which is why Omega will always be higher than alpha unless the items in question are true-score equivalent so all their factor loadings are the same. In this case then Alpha is the same as Omega.

EXPLORATORY FACTOR ANALYSIS

Our next chapter serves as the gateway into the rest of the book and all the different topics we'll be exploring together using this question format.

Personally, I have to admit Exploratory Factor Analysis and all the subtopics that fall under it are actually a lot more interesting than you ever thought possible. Due to exploratory factor analysis is arguably the statistical analysis technique that allows psychology to be a true science. Without exploratory factor analysis, we couldn't empirically say that X causes Y, we wouldn't have useful or valid scales or measurement tools to use in the real-world.

As an aspiring clinical psychologist, and as much as I don't want to admit this, I'm grateful that some extremely clever people came up with Exploratory Factor Analysis because it is this statistics that bridges the gap between psychological theory and applied psychology. This allows us to have valid measures for measuring mental health conditions and seeing if different psychological interventions help clients to improve their lives, decrease their psychological distress and use their more adaptive coping mechanisms.

Of course, I understand not everyone reading this is interested in clinical psychology, but Exploratory Factor Analysis is extremely useful in the real-world.

And that is certainly something I never ever thought I would say in a million years.

What is A Factorially Simple Variable?

This is a variable that indicates only one factor because this variable responds to changes in only a single factor as well as all but one of the factor loadings are 0.

What is A Factorially Complex Variable?

This is a variable that indicates more than one factor because it has several non-zero factor loadings and an example of this variable is a maths problem that involves both algebra and geometry.

In Terms Of Factorial Variables, What Is The Aim Of Most Psychological Measures?

In psychology, the aim of most psychological measures aim to create a set of factorially simple indicators also known as simple items from "independent clusters".

What Is An Exploratory Factor Analysis?

This is the process of finding a factor model that best explains the pattern of covariance between the observed variables in a given dataset. Therefore, an

Exploratory Factor Analysis finds a small set of factors that can be used to account for the covariances amongst the observed variables.

In addition, we need to remember that we can't run a factor analysis if none of the variables are uncorrelated (for example if none of the test items correlate because they don't measure the same attribute). As well as the simplest or parsimonious model should be preferred if a model with a larger number of factors doesn't fit any better than a model with a smaller number of factors.

What Is The Indeterminacy of Factor Loadings?

As a result of factor analysis procedures maximising the communalities and minimising the uniqueness in the loadings, this leaves us with some ambiguity about the exact values of the factor loadings. Since in a single-factor model, the same reproduced matrix with the same fit would be produced even if all the factor loadings switched signs. Due to in single-factor models the direction of the factor isn't identified so switching the sign doesn't change the model fit, variance or residuals explained in the model.

What Is A Rotation In Exploratory Factor Analysis?

Normally, a rotation is a transformation to achieve factorially simple variables.

What is The Rotation Problem?

Due to the directions of factor axes not being uniquely identified, this means that the rotation of axes result in a model having the same fit regardless of the rotation of the axes, but the factor loadings will be different.

How Do You Resolve The Rotation Problem?

The rotation problem is resolved by you assigning arbitrary positions and then you rotate them to approximate the given model. Normally, we do this because we're trying to get all the variables to a point where they are factorially simple, so they only load on one factor. Since these models are easier to interpret.

What is An Orthogonal Rotation?

In this type of rotation, the factors are assumed to be uncorrelated so the axes are independent from each other.

What is An Oblique Rotation?

Whereas in oblique rotations, the factors are allowed to be correlated, so the axes can be at oblique angles to each other.

What is The Varimax Rotation Method?

This is a type of orthogonal rotation method that minimises the number of variables that have high loadings on each individual factor, so this methods ends up simplifying the interpretation of factors for us.

What Is The Oblimin Rotation Method?

This is a default method in the R Studio package psych with its fa() function as this is an oblique rotation method so factors can be correlated with each other.

What is The Promax Rotation Method?

This is another oblique method that is useful for large models, because this rotation can be calculated quicker than a direct Oblimin rotation.

What Are The Best Practices For Exploratory Factor Analysis In Terms Of Sample Size?

In terms of sample size, it is best practice to have over 200 participants for an exploratory factor analysis with an a-priori rule of thumb being you should have at least 10 participants per variable. As well as the adequacy of your sample size can be determined by the nature of your data. For example, "strong data" would be a dataset with factor loadings of 0.7 or higher without any cross-loadings.

Whereas, larger sample sizes are needed to be able to confirm factor structures on "weak data" so you should need at least 20 participants per variable. Also, "weak data" can be characterised by having low factor loadings of at least 0.32 (Tabachinck & Fidell, 2001) and there are some cross-loading items where the loading is 0.32 or higher on two or more factors.

What Are The Two Methods Of Choice When It Comes To Extraction Factors?

You have the Methods Minimising Residuals which is the preferred choice when you have non-normal data or small samples. As well as you have the maximum likelihood method, which is effective for large samples and normally distributed data.

Why Should Oblique Rotations Always Be Preferred?

According to McDonald's Test Theory (1999), oblique rotations should always be preferred because for most applications, this type of rotation is conceptually sound, and even if the factors are found to be uncorrelated within one population, they still might be correlated in another population. Also, it's good to know that even if the factors are uncorrelated, the oblique rotation will still work fine and this rotation helps to avoid any identification problems with hidden "doublet" factors.

What Is A Doublet Factor?

A doublet factor refers to a problem that can happen amongst factors when there is one factor indicated by only two variables. Therefore, this is a problem because a factor model with two observed variables is not identified, and this is something I'll explain in another chapter.

However, when it comes to exploratory factor analysis with uncorrelated factors, the doublet-factor problem just can't be resolved with orthogonal rotations so these doublet factors are hidden from our analysis.

What Are The Purposes Of An Exploratory Factor Analysis?

An exploratory factor analysis helps us to decide how many factors underlie our data, interpret what these factors represent and most importantly, how these factors relate to each other.

Also, it is worth knowing, at one point it was

believed that exploratory factor analysis could help us "discover" new psychological constructs but this isn't true. Due to you cannot extract more factors than you put into the analysis, but you can learn about the nature of your data. For instance, you can find evidence for or against a hypothesized model and the analysis can give you hints of indications about the nature of the response processes that might be influencing your results.

What Is The Aim of A Principal Components Analysis?

A Principal Components Analysis aims to present the original variables through a smaller set of their linear combinations. Also, these components are weighted linear combinations of the original variables meaning the total number of the components are the same as the number of original variables in the analysis, but we can simplify our data by only retaining a few components with these components accounting for the most variances.

This is what makes it a data reduction technique.

How Does Principal Components Analysis Work?

The Principal Components Analysis works by the first component is the linear combination of the original variables that maximises the variance of the subjects' components scores. Then the second component is the one that maximises the remaining variance and it is uncorrelated with the first one, and this keeps happening until the number of components is equal to the number of original variables within the data.

How Would You Compare Principal Components Analysis And Factor Analysis?

These two statistics are very different from each other because Principal Components Analysis uses observed variables to form the component whereas factor analysis shows that the variables were caused by the factors, and factor analysis is a reflective model and Principal Components Analysis is a formative model.

In addition, Principal Components Analysis doesn't contain errors but factor analysis does contain errors, as well as within a factor analysis, the factors and errors are latent variables, whereas in a Principal Components Analysis all the variables are observed variables.

Should You Use Principal Components Analysis Or Factor Analysis?

Whilst Principal Components Analysis and factor analysis might seem similar and you might even get similar results when using them, they are still very, very different. For example, when you run these analyses on "weak" data, your results will be very different.

As a result of the components from Principal Components Analysis and factors from the factor analysis have different interpretations, because you use factor analysis when you're interested in the underlying attributes that cause a set of observed responses. This is what is used or needed in the vast majority of cases in psychology. Whereas in Principal Components Analysis, you use this when you're interested in forming new composite variables.

When Running an Exploratory Factor Analysis In R Studio, why do you need to add in sample size to the fa.parallel() function?

In R Studio, you need to add in your sample size or "number of observations" as an argument to the fa.parallel() function because this enables R Studio to run a stimulation of random data. As well as it's worth noting that R cannot tell from the correlation matrix alone how big the sample size is so we need to tell it. For example, you might use it as *fa.parallel(neo,* **n.obs=1000**, *fm="ml", fa="pc").*

Why is The fm=ml argument used In Exploratory Factor Analysis?

The problem with the fa.parallel() function is we need to change the default estimation method to maxmuim likelihood. Hence why we change it to "fm=ml" as well as we do this because the sample size is large and the scale scores are normally distributed. For example, *fa.parallel(neo, n.obs=1000***, fm="ml",** *fa="pc").*

Of course, this might not be applicable to your particular dataframe so check it first.

Why Is The fa="pc" argument used?

You use this argument when you want to tell R Studio to only show eigenvalues for principal components.

What Is The Default Number of Factors R Uses In The fa() function?

The default for the "number of factor" argument in the factor analysis function is 1, which is why you need to change it manual with the argument "nfactors=x" so it extracts however many number of factors you got from your scree plot (that's what x equals in that example).

How Do You Cut Out Factor Loadings In R Studio?

When doing an exploratory factor analysis, you might be dealing with a lot of variables and this can make the pattern matrix more than a little tedious to read. Therefore, you can "cut out" factor loadings under a particular size so you can focus on the larger and more important factor loadings. To do this you want to use the "print.psych()" function so if you ever wanted to cut out factor loadings smaller than 0.4 then you could use this code *print.psych(Emotion, cut=0.4)*.

CONFIRMATORY FACTOR ANALYSIS

Now that we have an understanding of Exploratory Factor Analysis, we're going to move onto the "big brother" of the last topic and onto Confirmatory Factor Analysis. This is another good topic because here we get introduced to Structural Equation Modelling.

This is a topic or an area of statistics that we're going to continue to focus on for a few chapters because it's made up of a few different areas. Yet each of them are important and they focus on slightly different areas of psychology research.

Therefore, even if you don't intend to become an academic and get heavily involved in research in the future (like me), you still need to be aware of this topic because if you're an applied psychologist like a clinical psychologist in the UK' National Health Service. Research is still going to be a focus for you and Confirmatory Factor Analysis will certainly be a valuable analysis tool and you can only use it if you know about it.

What Is Structural Equation Modelling?

This type of modelling takes a confirmatory approach to multivariate analysis because Structural Equation Modelling is an analysis of independencies and dependencies in a set of a common factors and/or measured variables.

What Other Names Has Structural Equation Modelling Been Known By?

There have been a lot of different names for Structural Equation Modelling over the decades including confirmatory factor analysis, path analysis, covariance structure modelling, latent variable modelling and unfortunately, causal modelling which isn't an accurate term at all.

In addition, the reason why these different names pop up is because they all reflect different aspects of Structural Equation Modelling but you need to know that Structural Equation Modelling is so much more than all of those individual components. Therefore, we call it Structural Equation Modelling because this encompasses all the new types of data and models that this statistical concept deals with, because the other names were just too narrow.

What Are Other Names For Observed (measured) Variables In Structural Equation Modelling?

Sometimes observed variables are called manifest variables, measures, indicators or proxies in Structural Equation Modelling with examples including well-being, weight and sex.

What Are Some Other Names Of Latent or Unobserved Variables?

In psychology latent variables tend to be called constructs, but they can be called latent traits and factors as well.

What Are Directional Paths In Structural Equation Modelling?

Within Structural Equation Modelling, directional paths always represent regression and there is only one equation per dependent variable, and the multiple sources of influence on the dependent variables are added in the equation as well as the regression coefficients are multipliers in the equation.

What Are Non-Directional Paths In Structural Equation Modelling?

Whereas non-directional paths correspond to covariances between variables so they don't show a directional relationship.

What Are Model Parameters?

According to Raykob and Marcoulides (2006), a parameter is a "generic term referring to a characteristic of a population such as mean or variance of a given variable,".

In addition, in Structural Equation Modelling, these parameters are the unknown aspects of the model and we're trying to investigate them, so they need to be estimated. For paths, we estimate the coefficients through the regression coefficients or covariances. Then for the variables, what we estimate depends on whether it is for our independent or dependent variable.

Lastly, every path or variance that hasn't been fixed needs to be estimated.

What Are Free Parameters?

These are parameters that are estimated or chosen based on theoretical ideas or experimental data itself instead of being predefined by the model.

What Are Fixed Parameters?

These are very different from fixed parameters because these parameters are completely defined by the model, because if X=5 then X is fixed at the value of 5.

What Are Constrained Parameters?

In addition, these "constraints parameters" are parameters that whilst they're restricted to an interval, they aren't completely defined. For instance, Y might be restricted to be a value between 0 and 1 but it isn't fixed to a specific value. This makes it a constricted in the model.

What Are Exogenous Variables?

This is another term for our independent variables because the changes in them are not explained by the model, so there are no directional arrows pointing to them. Also, the variance and mean of our independent variables are estimated.

What Are Endogenous Variables?

This is just a fancy way of saying dependent variables because these variables are influenced by other variables in the model, so there are directional arrows pointing to them. Also, these are written out as linear combinations of other variables and intercept is estimated, as well as the residual variance because the variance of a residual variable is attached to it.

Why Is Structural Equation Modelling Powerful?

Whilst you can do a lot of the traditional statistical tests within a Structural Equation Model anyway, like an ANOVA, mediation modelling and multiple regression. You actually start to understand just how powerful Structural Equation Modelling is when it comes to latent variables as you can do tests statistics like measurement by modelling and error-free variables where the measurement error is explicitly modelled.

As a result of measurement models allow researchers to infer measurement of latent variables from observed indicators (also known as measurement by modelling) and this forms the backbone of Structural Equation Modelling with latent variables.

This is another term for confirmatory factor analysis.

Furthermore, structural models mean researchers can model the relationships between latent variables or between latent and other observed variables that aren't included in measurement models.

Explain One Reason Why Confirmatory Factor Analysis Can Be Better Than Exploratory Factor Analysis

The problem with exploratory factor analysis is that it assumes that all factors load on all indicators and whilst we can sort of correct for this using rotations, these are still similar to "lucky draws". Whereas in a confirmatory factor analysis, we can test factor models that assume there are zero factor loadings for some indictors on some factors. Something that is impossible to test using exploratory factor analysis.

Overall, confirmatory factor analysis allow you to test any structure you like without the uncertainty that exploratory factor analysis gives you.

Why Do Latent Variables Need To Be Scaled?

Due to latent variables not having a natural scale, researchers need to give them a scale. Researchers can either set the variance to 1 because this makes them standardised variables, which is done often for common factors. Or they can adopt the unit of a measured variable, something that is always done for errors.

What Is An Absolute Goodness of Fit?

This is the discrepancy between the data at hand and the statistical model.

What Is The Goodness-Of-Fit Index?

This is a numerical summary of the discrepancy between the values expected and the observed values of a statistical model.

What Is The Goodness-Of-Fit Statistics?

This is a goodness-of-fit index with the known sampling distribution that might be used in a statistical-hypothesis testing.

What is Relative Goodness of Fit?

This is the discrepancy between two statistical models.

The source for the past four questions is Maydeu-Olivares and Garcia-Forero (2010).

Why Is Chi-Square A Goodness Of Fit Statistic?

This is a goodness-of-fit statistic because this tests the discrepancy between the expected values and observed values of a statistical model, and researchers want chi-square to be non-significant.

Also, if the sample size is large enough the chi-square test will reject the model as a result of very small discrepancies. Then similarly true, if your sample size is small then you can accept bad models by mistake.

What is The Comparative Fit Index?

This is an assessment of relative fit and it's used to compare the fit of a proposed model against another model that assumes that the variables are uncorrelated. This model is called the independence model.

Also, it might be worth noting that in R Studio, the independence model is based as the Baseline Model in the Lavaan package.

What Is The RMSEA?

This goodness-of-fit statistic stands for Root Mean Square Error of Approximation and this is tested against a known distribution and it computes confidence intervals too.

What Should You Do If You Have Large Differences Between Your Hypothesised Model And Observed Data?

Instead of panicking that this is the end of your research project, you can simply test other theoretical models, and the residuals will reveal the specific areas of misfit so you could address these areas with a modified model. Also, you can ask the program what model modifications would better fit your data. These are known as modification indices.

What Is A Modification Index?

A modification index is a chi-square change for a model where a constrained parameter is released.

What Are Two Sufficient Conditions Developed For Confirmatory Factor Analysis?

These basic rules follow the principles of identification of factor models so for each factor, there needs to be at least indicators that have zero loadings on all other factors and any factor that has only two defining indicators needs to be correlated with the other factor. As well as for each factor there are at least 3 indicators which have zero loadings on all other factors, so these are factorially simple.

When running a Confirmatory Factor Analysis In R Studio, How Do You Tell R What Items Measure A Variable?

Let's say you're looking at reasoning skills and this is measured by items f1, f2 and f3 on your scale or whatever you're using and you wanted to a confirmatory factor analysis on it. Then you would need to tell R using "+" that these items are linked together to measure the variable, and you would need to format it like a model in the following way:

Model <- ' Reasoning =~ f1 + f2 + f3
           Fluency =~ f4 + f5 + f6
           Language =~ f7 + f8 + f9 '

How Does Lavaan Scale Each Factor In R?

When it comes to scaling, the Lavaan package will scale each factor by assigning the same scale unit as the first indictor and the variance is then freely estimated. So if you we use the example above, because f1 is the first indictor, Lavaan will scale the rest of the Reasoning items to 1 and so on.

What Is The Confirmatory Factor Analysis Function In R Studio?

The confirmatory factor analysis function is cfa().

How Do You Make The cfa() Function Work?

If you use the cfa() function by itself, it won't do too much. Instead you need to name your model and the data so the code looks something like this *cfa(model= Model Name, data = Data Frame Name).*

In addition, most of the time, you can just use that because R will be dealing with the raw data in a subject-by-variable data frame. Yet sometimes you will need to augment the code to account for the dataframe being taken from a sample covariance or correlation matrices. If this happens then you use code similar to *fit <- cfa(model=T.model, sample.cov=Dataframe, sample.nobs=300)*

How Do You Standardise All Latent Variables?

If you need to change how your latent variables are scaled by you can add std.lv=TRUE to your code. Like this, *Model.2 <- cfa(T.model, sample.cov=Dataframe, sample.nobs=300, std.lv=TRUE)*

How Do You Get The Standardised Solution?

If you want everything to be standardised including the observed as well as latent variables, then you need to add *standardised=TRUE* to your summary() function output. For instance, *summary(Model2, standardised=TRUE)*

How Do You Request The Fitted Covariance Matrix?

In R Studio, you need to use the fitted() function. Such as *fitted(model2)*.

How Do You Get The Residuals And What Are They?

The residuals are the differences between the actual and fitted observed covariances and you use the *residual()* function. As seen in *residual(model2)*. Then if you want the standardised residuals then you add on *type="standardised"* within the brackets.

How Do You Request The Modification Indices?

Lastly, you can just use the *modindices()* function to use the modification indices. Such as *modindices(Model2)*.

PATH ANALYSIS

Continuing with our investigation into Structural Equation Modelling, path analysis is another good area to look at. Especially, with path analysis not needing any common factors and instead this type of Structural Equation Modelling focuses on the relationship between observed variables and how they relate to the predictions of dependent variables.

In other words, you can do some very interesting and cool stuff with path analysis that you can't do with Confirmatory Factor Analysis.

Let's start exploring our next topic.

What Is Path Analysis?

Path Analysis is Structural Equation Modelling without any common factors because it is an analysis of the relationships between observed variables with this analysis being interested in causal systems. In other words, how do independent variables relate with the predictions of dependent variables. Also, path analysis looks at distal causes on dependent variables caused by indirect effects, as well as proximal causes of dependent variables.

In addition, it's worth noting that just because common factors aren't used in path analysis, we still need residuals (which are latent variables) since these allow for influences that we cannot explain within our model.

How Did Path Analysis Originate?

Sewall Wright (1921) conducted an analysis on causality in behavioural genetics and because he wasn't happy with all partial correlations, he developed path analysis. This is a special case of Structural Equation Modelling.

At the time, statisticians were interested in path analysis and even applied biologists preferred Fisher's methods because they were easier to understand and rooted in experimental design (Shipley, 2000).

What Are Direct Effects?

Simply put this is when X causes Y.

What Are Indirect Effects?

This is when X causes M which leads to causes Y.

What Are Spuriousness Effects?

This effect type is when Z causes X and Y.

What Is An Unexplained Co-Variation Relationship Between Two Variables?

This is when both X and Y are exogenous variables, so they're both independent variables and they aren't impacted by the model.

What Is The Basis Of Path Analysis?

Regression forms the basis for path analysis but this is somewhat problematic considering that regression is only interested in explaining variance in the dependent variable and establishing independent effects of predictors controlling for other predictors. This has nothing to do with causality since regression models don't even consider or assume it.

What Are Multiple Regression Models?

Linking to the question above, this is why we need multiple regression models because we want to know about variance and the independent effects, but we want to know more. Granted we don't want to know the reasons for the relationships between the predictors, because we assume that all independent variables are potentially related and their covariances are freely estimated.

The answer to this question is continued below.

What Are Saturated Models?

Therefore, we need multiple regression models because we can examine a large number of parameters on a dependent variable. This is where saturated regression models come in too when the number of parameters is equal to the number of sample moments so every observed variable is connected to every other observed variable.

This is a little problematic because we can identify this model but we can't test it because there is nothing to test. Also, the model is as complicated as the original variables so the regression simply presents the observed variance and the covariances between the variables as the covariances and variances of the independent variables and regression coefficients.

What Are Path Models?

A path model is a composite hypothesis made up of omitted directional as well as non-directional paths. This means that unlike multiple regression models there are some omitted directional paths so the influence is restricted to mediation through specific pathways and omitted non-directional paths. This means that further common causes don't exist.

Overall, Path Models allow you to test multiple complex hypothesis at the same time.

What Are The Two Levels Of Significance Testing In Path Models?

The first level is when you test the significance of individual model parameters, like in a specific regression coefficient significant. Also, this first level works on saturated models too.

Secondly, you can test the significance of the goodness of fit of the overall model to the observed data so this is where you compare the "model predicted" covariances with the observed covariances using a Chi-Square test. If all the covariances are included in the model then the model will be saturated so they'll be nothing to test. Hence, the aim is to test the hypothesis with restrictions on the relationships between the variables.

Why Isn't Goodness of Fit Useful In Path Analysis?

According to McDonald (1999), researchers seem to rely a lot on goodness-of-fit indices and McDonald argues that "actual discrepancies" or residuals are a lot more informative to researchers. Which makes sense because global indices of fit as we saw in the last chapter, aren't informative in path analysis.

As a result, if we take Standardised Root Mean Square Residual, for example, in path analysis this makes little sense because path analysis allows direct covariances paths and this reproduces correlations for them to be exact. Hence, if we did use that indices and average a lot of 0 residuals with a few non-zero ones then this will give us a false impression that the model fits well.

What Are Recursive Path Models?

This is a type of path model that is recursive if no chain of directional paths form a closed loop with McDonald (1999) writing "Mutual or reciprocal causations present some deep problems in philosophy of science. It is difficult to conceive that two variables simultaneously determine each other's values. A closed loop can represent either a system of dynamic processes that have come into equilibrium with each other at the time the measurements are taken, or a cross section of what should better have been observed as a recursive system changing over intervals of time."

What Is An Autoregressive Model?

This type of statistical model focuses on "time series" data or, in other words, how different variables change or remain the same at different points of measurement. For example, you would use an autoregressive model when looking at differences in intelligence between Measurement Time 1 and Measurement Time 2.

Due to an autoregressive model describes how an observation is depended on one or more preceding observations, to different extents. Hence, using our intelligence test example, an autoregressive model shows how the current value of a participant's intelligence is influenced by its own past values.

What Are The Advantages Of Path Analysis?

Path analysis allows researchers to test more complex and more realistic models as well as path analysis are more flexible and powerful than more traditional statistics especially when we want to deal with a lot of dependent variables or mediation.

What Are The Disadvantages Of Path Analysis?

The main disadvantages of path analysis are that it open to abuse as some people will claim that path analysis show causality but this isn't true. You cannot establish causality based on the model fit. Also, experiments are not better than Structural Equation Modelling because longitudinal and experimental data can be much better modelled as well as tested using structural equation modelling.

Moreover, path analysis assumes that observed

variables don't have measurement error, which is wrong so it's important not to mix the residuals from imperfect predictions with the error of measurement. Hence, why it is important that variables in path analysis are measured very, very accurately.

When It Comes To Writing Models, How Do You Tell R Studio One Variable Is Regressed Onto Another One?

To do this you will need to use the ~ symbol because this tells R that one factor is regressed onto another one. For instance, if your variable K is regressed onto P and Z then you would need to write this out as "K ~ P + Z" into R Studio.

How Would You Tell R Studio Something Is Correlated With Another Variable When Writing Out Your Model?

When you want to tell R Studio that one variable is correlated with another variable or the covariances will be, you need to you the ~~ symbol in your model. For example, if you wanted to tell R Studio that the covariances of P and Z will be correlated then you would write *P* ~~ Z.

Also, it's important that you do this correlation of covariances for both your independent and dependent variables.

How Would You Write Out A Full Model In R Studio?

Presumably you would be given a graphic of your theoretical model so you can see which variables regress onto each other and what covariances should correlate. Then using what you can see in the graphic, you can use your ~ and ~~ symbols to write out your model in a way that R studio can understand.

For example, *T.Model <- K ~ P + Z*
A ~ O + G
H ~ J + W
P ~~ Z
O ~~ G
J ~~ W'

What Function Do You Use To Fit Path Models?

To fit path models, you use the sem() function.

Once You Get The Basic sem() and Chi-Square Output, How Do You Get The Extended Output?

In case you want to see the more detailed output, you need to assign this to a new object in R Studio and then request the extended output by using code similar to the following example:

fit <- sem(Model Name, sample.cov=Wellbeing, sample.nobs=200)

summary(fit, fit.measures=TRUE)

How Do You Interpret Residual Correlations?

Since residuals are actual correlations from the correlation matrix, we can think of them as differences between two sets of correlations so similar to correlations of 0.1. We can give of any residual correlations of 0.1 as small and anything below that as trivial.

How Do You Tell If Any Standardised Residuals Are Statistically Significant?

You should request standardised residuals

because you want to test if any of the residuals are significantly difference from 0 and if you have any standardised residuals larger than 1.96 (basically 2 standard deviations away from the mean in the standard normal distribution) then they're significantly different from 0 at a confidence interval of 0.05.

To get the standardised residuals you can use this code *residuals(Object Name, type="standardized")*

FULL STRUCTURAL EQUATION MODELLING

Originally, I had *why does this topic deserve its own chapter* as one of the questions but because I accidentally ended up with 402 questions for this book. Thankfully, I can afford to get rid of it to form an easy introduction to this next chapter.

Therefore, we need to talk about full structural models in Structural Equation Modelling separately because in the past two chapters, we've looked at confirmatory factor analysis and path analysis. Both of these are special cases of Structural Equation Modelling, so in this chapter we're going to be putting them together to create full structural models.

What Is A Cross-lagged Latent Autoregressive Model?

This is an autoregressive model that looks at the influences from other constructs that have been previously measured.

What Are Nested Models?

You have nested models when you have one model that is a special case of the other as well as both models absolutely must have the same observed variables, and one model can be obtained from the other by fixing one or more free parameters.

What Is Differential Item Functioning?

Differential Item Functioning, sometimes shortened to DIF, is the statistical property of a test item that shows how likely it is for respondents from different groups that possess similar abilities to respond differently to the test item.

Another way to explain it is that Differential Item Functioning basically refers to people from different groups with similar skill levels, don't have an equal chance of answering a question correctly.

This is something we explore in the following chapters and questions.

What Are Some Ways To Assess Differential Item Functioning?

You can assess Differential Item Functioning using logistic regression, confirmatory factor analysis as well as Item Response Theory, because these are the methods we'll look at in this book.

Yet you can assess Differential Item Functioning using the Mantel-Haenszel procedure too, but this isn't something we look at.

Why Is Detecting And Addressing Differential Item Functioning Important?

You need to detect and address Differential Item Functioning because this ensures a fair and unbiased assessment and test items.

How Do You Know Which Model Is The More Restrictive One?

When you need to test the difference between nested models, you can tell which one is the more restrictive model because it will have free parameters that become fixed. Meaning the more restrictive model has fewer parameters compared to the other one or ones.

Why Does The More Restrictive Model Always Have a Higher Chi-Square?

As a result of you increasing the number of parameters, this makes the model more relaxed so it fits the data easier. Hence, the more restrictive model just can't fit better than the less restrictive model and this is why the more restrictive model always has the higher chi-square result.

Also, this means the difference in the chi-square result between both these models is always positive.

What Is The Rule Of Parsimony?

This is where if there is no statistical difference between the two models, we always choose the more restrictive or "simpler" model over the other one.

How Do You Tell If The Two Models Have A Statistical Difference?

You need to look at the difference in the chi-square is distributed as chi-square. Since

$\Delta\chi2 = \chi2\text{more restrictive} - \chi2\text{less restrictive}$

$\Delta df = df \text{ more restrictive} - df \text{ less restrictive}$

As a result if the $\Delta\chi2$ test is significant then the two models are significantly different.

What Are Some Examples Of Nested Models?

Three examples of nested models include some factor models that have the same number of indicators, because a one-factor model is nested within a model with more factors. As well as a model with orthogonal factors is nested within a model with correlated factors.

In addition, the independence model is nested within any model.

Finally, any model is nested within a saturated model.

Why Do We Care About The Mean Structure For Longitudinal Studies?

We need to bring the means of latent factors (also known as mean structure) as well as intercepts into our model when looking at longitudinal studies because they help us to see how much of the measured values change on average. Hence, this allows us to answer the question of absolute growth and this isn't something we can get from covariances between measures (something we've only been looking at until now) due to covariances only measure how well the relative ordering of respondents is preserved.

How Can The Observations Be Described When A Developmental *Process* is of interest To Researchers?

We can describe observations as trajectories of change. Since in a developmental process context for a child, we can consider the slope and the intercept of the process. Since these two are latent variables so every child can be described by their own standing on the intercept and slope variables as well as we might assume the slope and intercept are normally distributed.

This is part of the topic of latent growth curve models.

What Is Measurement Invariance Across Time?

This is when the same score on the latent construct results in the same expected scores for its indicators whether these are items, subtests or the test itself.

Why Is Measurement Invariance Important?

Using the discussion from Horn (1991), let's suppose we ask participants who are 20 years old and 70 years old something along the lines of:

- Do you feel you are as good looking as the average person?
- Do you feel you are every bit as smart as the average person?

- Do you feel you are liked by others as much as the average person is liked?

The problems researchers would face is that they can't simply add up the item scores to give them a valid measure in a longitudinal design. Therefore, we need to ensure measurement invariance across time so our tests provide equivalent measurement over time. In other words, we need to make sure the origin and unit of our measurement stays the same.

How Do You Ensure You Have The Same Unit And Origin Of Measurement Across Time?

To make sure that you have the same unit and original of measurement across time, you need to keep some of the same indicators to basically "link" the scales of your constructs. As a result, whilst I cannot put an illustration into this book, if you look at diagrams surrounding this topic you'll see that measurement at different Times share the same indictors.

Therefore, this provides time-invariant measures because by constraining the shared indictors you end up with the same parameters (factor loadings and intercepts) across time. This thankfully fixes the scale of your measurement equally across time.

What Is Construct Equivalence?

This is where the same psychological constructs are measured across time.

What Is Measurement Unit Equivalence?

Here, you have the same measurement unit across time so you can investigate individual differences found at Time 1 and compare them against individual differences found at Time 2.

What Is Scalar Equivalence?

With scalar equivalence, you have the same measurement unit and origin and often you have the same SEm as well. This allows you to compare the scores across time.

R Questions For Full Structural Models

What R Packages Do You Need To Test Full Structural Models?

You'll need the Lavaan package to test your structural equation models and the psych package is useful to activate too in case you need descriptive statistics for your exam.

How Would You Write A Model In R Studio Using Multiple Subscales (Indicators) To Measure A Factor?

This is nice and simple for a change because if you have a factor, let's call it, Depression, and it's measured and regressed by three subscales then you need to tell R Studio using the ~ symbol.

For example: *Model1 <- 'Depression =~ p1_Happy + p1_Sad + p1_Mood'*

I've made up the subscale names but you see how you tell R that the three subscales are regressed onto the factor.

How Would You Write A Model Using Multiple Subscales And Times Of Measurement?

Again, you would need to look at your model and write it out so R Studio knows your model has three different subscales that measure behaviour at two different times. For instance, *Model1 <- 'Depression =~ p1_Happy + p1_Sad + p1_Mood*

Depression2 =~ p2_Happy + p2_Sad + p2_Mood

Depression ~ Depression2'

You need to include the last bit about Depression being regressed on Depression2 because the model is arguing that Depression2 is linearly dependent on Depression.

How Are Factors Scaled By Default In R Studio?

By default, in R Studio, your factors will be scaled by adopting the scale of their first indicator and the loadings will be of the first indicator too. So if you want the scale and loadings to be different, you need to manually change it.

If You're Interested In The Change Between Time Measures, What Do You Need To Do In R?

If you're interested in the change between Time 1 and Time 2 of a measurement, you need to bring the means and intercepts into the analysis, and the easiest way to do this is to add *meanstructure=TRUE* in your sem() function and then requesting the outputs.

Such as *fit0 <- sem(model = Model0, data = SDQ, meanstructure=TRUE)*

summary(fit0, fit.measures=TRUE)

How Do You Specify Labels For Path Coefficients?

Sometimes known as factor loadings because they are the same as path coefficients, you need to add multipliers in front of any indicators that you need labels for. For example, *1K*p1_Happy*.

How Do You Specify Labels For Intercepts?

When it comes to specifying the labels for intercepts, you need to use multipliers in statements of ~ 1 so if you wanted to write the intercept for p1_Happy then you would write *p1_Happy ~ ih*1*

MULITPLE-GROUP STRUCTURAL EQUATION MODELLING

Now we need to switch this topic on its head slightly, because so far we've only looked at what happens or how we do Structural Equation Modelling for a single group. For example, male or females and not both. Yet there are times in psychology research when we do want to look at multiple groups and this allows us to draw conclusions between them.

For instance, one example I've seen in the literature is something along the lines of multiple-group structural equation modelling has allowed researchers to understand that for every 1 point increase for males, there is an X times increased chance of a diagnosis compared to females, where for every 1 point increase, there is a Y decreased chance of a diagnosis. Then you can imply gender effects and talk all about these differences.

As a result, multiple-group Structural Equation Modelling is a powerful next step in our learning and our research.

Why Use Multiple-Group Structural Equation Modelling?

Since it allows you to analyse data from samples of different populations because if you hypothesize that there will be a moderating effect on a regression or correlation coefficient then interaction variables need to be created. And the different cases of Structural Equation Modelling that we've looked at so far have used group variable (a dummy coded variable) as a "covariate" to look at the differences between groups.

This isn't appropriate now.

Hence the need for Multiple-Group Structural Equation Modelling.

What Sort Of Research Questions Would Multiple-Group Structural Equation Modelling Be Useful For?

You might want to use Multiple-Group Structural Equation Modelling when looking at the whether the means of latent constructs are the same in boys and girls, or whether the rate of change in symptoms are different for treatment and placebo groups in your study or whether the process of participating in sports is the same for children in collectivistic or individualistic societies.

Overall, Multiple-Group Structural Equation Modelling can be useful when looking at a process, rate of change or latent "something" (be it variable or factor) based research question.

What Questions Does Multiple-Group Structural Equation Modelling Seek To Answer?

In a boarder sense, we can use Multiple-Group Structural Equation Modelling to answer questions about the similarities and differences in latent constructs. Therefore, we can understand the validity of a measurement model in each group and we can establish this model. For example, we can see whether members of different groups give the same meaning to items and questions, or the same meaning to the construct that we're investigating.

Equally, Multiple-Group Structural Equation Modelling helps us to answer questions about measurement invariance because we can see if measurement invariance holds then substantive comparisons can be made between the groups, and if it doesn't hold then the groups aren't be compared so we need to make adjustments.

On the whole, factor models just provide us with a very nice and convenient framework to operationalise measurement invariance.

What Is Measurement Invariance?

A measure is invariant across your different groups when members of these different groups with the same true score are expected to have the same observed sores. As well as the definition of measurement invariance implies that after we control for the true score, the test score just shouldn't depend on the group that the respondent belongs too.

Also, when it comes to item score, a violation of

measurement invariant does constitute as Differential Item Functioning.

What is Configural Invariance?

To have configural invariance, you need to have the same factor model specification holding across the different groups. This means you have to have the same number of factors and loading patterns across the groups.

What Is Metric Invariance?

To have metric invariance, you need equal factor loadings across your different groups to ensure the same scale unit. This allows you to compare the differences between respondents across the groups and you can compare factor variances across the groups as well.

What Is Scalar Invariance?

You have scalar invariance when you have equal intercepts across the different groups because this ensures you have the same scale origin so you can compare respondent's scores and factor means across the different groups.

When Do You Have Uniform Differential Item Functioning In Violations Of Measurement Invariance?

When uniform Differential Item Functioning is present, you'll see that one of your groups has a lower or higher expected item score across all levels of the factor score (True Score). Therefore, this is the main effect of Group on the observed item score.

When Do You Have Non-Uniform Differential Item Functioning In Violations Of Measurement Invariance?

On the other hand, when non-uniform Differential Item Functioning is present, you'll see one of your groups has a higher expected item score in one area of the factor score (again, True Score) distribution, as well as lower expected item score in other areas. Hence, this is the interaction effect of True Score x Group on the observed item score.

What Is Unique Variance Invariance?

You have unique variance invariance when you have equal unique error variances as these ensure the same error of measurement, as well as this precludes systematic sources of error are affecting the score differently across your groups.

When is There Enough Power To Detect Measurement Invariance Violations?

By their use of simulations, Lubke and Dolan (2003) manage to show that when all measurement parameters are constrained to be equal, this results in their being enough power to detect all measurement invariance violations. This isn't possible when residual variance isn't held equal.

What Is Weak Invariance?

This is another term seen in the statistics literature and weak invariance requires you to have cross-equality in the loadings.

What Is Strong Invariance?

You have strong invariance when you have cross-group equality in the intercepts and loadings.

What Is Strict Invariance?

You'll have strict invariance when you have cross-group equality in the residual variances, intercepts and loadings. As well as Meredith (1993) argued that strict invariance is a needed condition for a fair and equitable comparison.

What Do You Do When You Have Non-Invariance?

You can adjust for non-invariance in your measurement models by doing a few simple things. You need to release the parameter constraints for non-invariant items so the latent factors will be corrected for the non-invariance and you can use partially invariant models for substantive conclusions and scoring.

What's The Purpose Of Measurement Invariance Studies?

According to Zumbo (2007), we can use measurement invariance studies to try and understand item response processes, investigate the lack of invariance, investigate the comparability of adapted and/ or translated measures, investigate equity and fairness in an assessment and to deal with a possible threat to internal validity. For example, to rule out a measurement artifact as an explanation for the group differences.

Why Are Translated Tests Psychometrically Difficult?

It's common sense to know that we translate different psychometric tests into different languages and adapt them so they can be used in different cultures as well as countries. Yet, there is a very real risk that respondents are unfairly disadvantaged by the translated test because they're not part of the culture the original test was designed for. Since verbal things present us with translation issues, non-verbal items are open to culturally specific interpretations or the respondent might have a disadvantage related to the testing procedure or an additional nuisance factor.

Then even from a theoretical viewpoint, it's very hard to prove that two measurements have a common unit or origin measurement.

When You Want To Fit A Model For Different Groups, How Do You Do That?

To fit a model, you need to use the cfa() function but because you don't want to run the analysis on the whole sample, you want to run the analysis on separate groups, you need to tell R there is a grouping variable in use.

For example, your code might look like *fit1 <- cfa(Model Name, data = Data Name, group = "sex")*

As a result, our model will be fitted to both groups instead of the sample as a whole without parameter constraints.

Do You Need To Do Anything To Get Means And Intercepts For Multiple-Group Analysis?

No, because these are included as standard when you run multiple-group analysis.

How Do You Get Certain Parameters To Be Equal For Every Corresponding Test Between Groups?

To get an invariance model that will allow you to compare factor scores across different groups properly, you need to make the residual variances, intercepts and factor loadings equal across your different groups.

Therefore, in Lavaan, you only need to add the parameters you want to equal using the argument *group.equal*.

As a result, your code should look something like this *fit2 <- cfa(Model Name, data = Data Name, group = "sex", group.equal = c("loadings", "intercepts", "residuals")*

Multiple-Group Structural Equation Modelling

Why Use Multiple-Group Structural Equation Modelling?

Since it allows you to analyse data from samples of different populations because if you hypothesize that there will be a moderating effect on a regression or correlation coefficient then interaction variables need to be created. And the different cases of Structural Equation Modelling that we've looked at so far have used group variable (a dummy coded variable) as a "covariate" to look at the differences between groups.

This isn't appropriate now.

Hence the need for Multiple-Group Structural Equation Modelling.

What Sort Of Research Questions Would Multiple-Group Structural Equation Modelling Be Useful For?

You might want to use Multiple-Group Structural Equation Modelling when looking at the whether the means of latent constructs are the same in boys and girls, or whether the rate of change in symptoms are different for treatment and placebo groups in your study or whether the process of participating in sports is the same for children in collectivistic or individualistic societies.

Overall, Multiple-Group Structural Equation Modelling can be useful when looking at a process, rate of change or latent "something" (be it variable or factor) based research question.

What Questions Does Multiple-Group Structural Equation Modelling Seek To Answer?

In a boarder sense, we can use Multiple-Group Structural Equation Modelling to answer questions about the similarities and differences in latent constructs. Therefore, we can understand the validity of a measurement model in each group and we can establish this model. For example, we can see whether members of different groups give the same meaning to items and questions, or the same meaning to the construct that we're investigating.

Equally, Multiple-Group Structural Equation Modelling helps us to answer questions about measurement invariance because we can see if measurement invariance holds then substantive comparisons can be made between the groups, and if it doesn't hold then the groups can't be compared so we need to make adjustments.

On the whole, factor models just provide us with a very nice and convenient framework to operationalise measurement invariance.

When is There Enough Power To Detect Measurement Invariance Violations?

By their use of simulations, Lubke and Dolan (2003) manage to show that when all measurement parameters are constrained to be equal, this results in their being enough power to detect all measurement invariance violations. This isn't possible when residual variance isn't held equal.

What Is Weak Invariance?

This is another term seen in the statistics literature and weak invariance requires you to have cross-equality in the loadings.

What Is Strong Invariance?

You have strong invariance when you have cross-group equality in the intercepts and loadings.

What Is Strict Invariance?

You'll have strict invariance when you have cross-group equality in the residual variances, intercepts and loadings. As well as Meredith (1993) argued that strict invariance is a needed condition for a fair and equitable comparison.

Multiple-Group Structural Equation Modelling R Questions

When You Want To Fit A Model For Different Groups, How Do You Do That?

To fit a model, you need to use the cfa() function but because you don't want to run the analysis on the whole sample, you want to run the analysis on separate groups, you need to tell R there is a grouping variable in use.

For example, your code might look like *fit1 <- cfa(Model Name, data = Data Name, group = "sex")*

As a result, our model will be fitted to both groups instead of the sample as a whole without parameter constraints.

Do You Need To Do Anything To Get Means And Intercepts For Multiple-Group Analysis?

No, because these are included as standard when you run multiple-group analysis.

How Do You Get Certain Parameters To Be Equal For Every Corresponding Test Between Groups?

To get an invariance model that will allow you to compare factor scores across different groups properly, you need to make the residual variances, intercepts and factor loadings equal across your different groups.

Therefore, in Lavaan, you only need to add the parameters you want to equal using the argument *group.equal*.

As a result, your code should look something like this *fit2 <- cfa(Model Name, data = Data Name, group =*

"sex", group.equal = c("loadings", "intercepts", "residuals")

LOGISTIC REGRESSION

The final topic in our look at Structural Equation Modelling, we're going to be exploring logistic regression. Whilst I admit this topic took me a little while (a long while) to get my head around, this chapter spares you the worst of that and judging by our psychology masters group chat a lot of my fellow students found this topic to be very difficult too.

Although, logistic regression deals with an extremely useful and critical part of psychology research. It deals with dichotomous variables, which can be considered the bread-and-butter of certain areas of psychology. Therefore, it is critical that there is a way to perform Structural Equation Modelling on these variables because of the problems I talk about below.

What Is The Problem With Measuring Dichotomous Variables?

The problem is that so far in this book of questions, we've looked at correlational techniques that assume that our variables are continuous. Like linear regression as well as factor analysis both assume that we are dealing with continuous variables.

In addition, even when dealing with binary items that are dichotomous by their very nature, we can overcome the problem by using tetrachoric correlations and then we can use our linear correlation techniques on them.

However, when it comes to truly dichotomous variables, these methods aren't good or useful.

As a result, we need to use logistic regression (which in itself is only one method for doing this) because it allows us to extend test theory and our measurement models to categorical observations.

What Are Dichotomised Latent Continua?

Sometimes you'll have dichotomous variables that are dichotomised latent continua. For instance "Agree or Disagree" and for these binary items, we use tetrachoric correlations because Pearson's correlations help us to understand the relationship between latent response tendencies and our observations.

What Are Some Examples of Dichotomous Outcomes?

Some examples of dichotomous outcomes include:

- Yes Or No for whether a client dropped out of therapy

- Yes or No for an employee staying in a new job after 6 months
- Survival
- Malignant or Benign Tumour for a diagnosis
- Rejection or Job Offer for the outcome of job selection.

What Is The Purpose of Analysing Dichotomous Outcomes?

We analyse dichotomous outcome variables to assess the effects of multiple different exploratory variables on a dichotomous outcome variable.

Why Don't Linear Models Work For Dichotomous Outcomes?

When you try to fit a linear regression model to predicting a dichotomous outcome variable, like cancer survival, it won't work. Due to the predicted outcome isn't bound so it takes values less than 0 and greater than 1 and it takes non-integer values (like decimal points) into account so the fit just doesn't work.

This is why your predicted outcome needs to be dichotomised.

Why Is Probability Another Way To Think About This Sort Of Data?

You can think about this sort of data in terms of probability because instead of predicting a certain outcome, researchers are trying to predict its probability. The probability of an event is estimated from the proportion of the event occurring out of all possible outcomes as well as as the sample size increases, the proportion will approach probability.

Also, probability is divided up into different bands of probability so this helps to solve the bounding issue faced in linear models.

What Are Conditional Means?

This is where the mean outcome is conditional on the predictor.

Why Does A Non-Linear Function Predict Probability?

As mentioned earlier, because probability has an increasing number of bands, the conditional means will approach an s-shaped curve which is useful for our intereption compared to linear models. Also, as probability increases, our dichotomous outcome variable increases too but it is ultimately bound between 0 and 1.

Still, we need a formulation for this non-linear function so we can use it in our prediction.

What Are Odds= P/(1-P)?

Odds= P/(1-P) is the ratio of probability of an event occurring to the probability of the same event not occurring.

What Are Log Odds?

Log odds are the natural logarithm of the odds and this used to convert odds to a continuous scale, so we can use dichotomous data in linear models.

In addition, log odds are used in the logistic regression to model the relationship between the predictor variable or variables and a dichotomous outcome variable.

How Do You Interpret Log Odds?

When you get the results of Log Odds, they'll be in coefficients and a positive coefficient means there's an increase in the odds of success or an event occurring. Then if you have a negative coefficient then there is a higher chance of the event not occurring.

How Is Logistic Regression Similar To Linear Regression?

These two statistical methods are similar because you can use both to do hierarchical model testing and both are helpful for investigating the significance of the model overall as well as the individual predictors.

How Is Logistic Regression Different To Linear Regression?

Although, these two methods are difference because the Odds are log transformed, and instead of predicting the value of Y from X like you do in linear regression, in logistic regression, you predict the log odds of Y given X.

What Is The Most Convenient Way To Code Binary Outcomes?

The best way to code binary outcomes is when the keyed or target outcome, which is the outcome you're interested in, is coded as 1. Since any positive effect means that the independent variable is positively related to the keyed outcome, and any negative effect means the independent variable is negative related to the keyed outcome.

What Is An Additive Model?

In an additive model, this model represents the arithmetic sum of the predictor variables' individual effects. Therefore, an additive model considers the sum of the effects.

What Is A Multiplicative Model?

Whereas this model involves multiplying the predictor's variables' effects. Consequently, this type of model accounts for interactions through its use of multiplication.

Why Do We Need To Calculate exp(B) For Logistic Regression?

We need to do this because our regression coefficient is interpreted as odds rather than log odds, so we need to calculate exp(B) for our logistic regression. Since when we know exp(B), we'll be able to know the ratio of odds corresponding to a 1-point increase in the predictor.

How Do You Interpret Regression Coefficient (B) For Logistic Regression?

Once you have your B coefficient, you'll be able to see that if your Odds ratio is less than 1, your predictor will decrease the odds of outcome occurring. If your Odds ratio is 0 then your predictor doesn't change the odds of the outcome occurring. Finally, if your Odds Ratio is greater than 1 then the predictor increases the odds of the outcome occurring.

What Is The Advantage Of Multiple Regression Over Simple Regression?

By using multiple regression, you're able to include all your variables into your model, something you can't do with a simple regression. Also, the regression coefficients are interpreted in the same way as in a linear regression because your B_1 increased in log odds when X_1 increases by 1 point with all the other predictors held constant.

What Is Logistic Function?

A logistic function is the probability of a respondent responding correctly given the total score. Also, when we say "correctly" we don't really care about the answer itself, because psychometrically, we only care if the participant was able to pass the item.

When Thinking About Differential Item Functioning, What Should Equal Ability Result In?

Equal ability or any other trait that your test is measuring should result in respondents from both groups having an equal probability of passing the item.

What Equation Is Used When You Want To Test The Model Predicting The Probability of A Correct Answer From The Trait Level?

The equation used here is $log_e(odds) = B_0 + B_1 Trait$

What Do You Need To Add To The Equation To Check For Uniform DIF?

You would need to add the Group variable to the regression so it would look like this $log_e(odds) = B_0 + B_1 Trait + B_2 Group$

What About For Checking Non-Uniform DIF?

Then you would need to add in the interaction term between the group and trait variables. For example, $log_e(odds) = B_0 + B_1 Trait + B_2 Group \times Group$.

What Is The Nagelkerke R^2 Statistic?

This statistic refers to the logistic regression effect size and this allows us to compare the effect size to other models. As well as Nagelkerke R^2 statistic is better than other R-square alternatives, like Cox & Snell, because it can achieve a value of 1, at least in theory.

How Do You Interpret DIF Decisions And Effect Sizes?

You can use these guidelines from Jodin and Gierl (2001):

- Negligible DIF

Chi square insignificant **or**
Nagelkerke R^2 change < 0.035

- Moderate DIF

Chi square significant **and**
Nagelkerke R^2 change between 0.035 and 0.07

- Large DIF

Chi square significant **and**
Nagelkerke R^2 change ≥ 0.07

What Is Item Bias?

You can have item bias when respondents from your two groups don't have an equal chance of passing an item because some of the characteristics of the item aren't relevant to the construct you're measuring.

What's The Link Between DIF And Item Bias?

In order to have item bias, you need to have DIF but this doesn't tell the whole story. Since if you don't have DIF then you don't have any item bias, but if DIF is present in your model, then you need to investigate further. Due to you need to see if these discrepancies that cause DIF to develop are caused by your test item or an irrelevant characteristic of your examinees.

Logistic Regression R Studio Questions

Why Is The EPQ Unusual For A Personality Questionnaire?

The EPQ, or Eysenck Personality Questionnaire, is a little strange for a personality questionnaire because it doesn't use Likert scales to boost the amount of information it can get from respondents. Instead it uses tons of binary test items to ensure it has a good content coverage, so we need to use logistic regressions to analyse this data.

Why Is The Sex Variable Critical For DIF Analysis?

It's critical because DIF is all about investigating if different groups with similar abilities have an unequal chance of passing a test item, so looking at the sex variable will help you to clearly see a difference, if it exists.

In Binary Test Items, How Do You need Which Is The Focus Group?

Whatever group is coded as 1 is the focal group.

When There Are Some Missing Item Responses, How Do You Compute The Sum Score?

You can use the base R function of rowMeans() to compute the average item score and you need to omit the NA values from the calculation so you use the na.rm=TRUE argument. Then you multiply this by whatever the number of items is in your scale. Also, when it comes to the column numbers in your code, these are the columns of the trait scale you're focusing on.

For example, your code would look something like this:

EPQ$Nscore <- rowMeans(EPQ[,4:26], na.rm=TRUE)*23

How Would You Code A Variable Like Sex In R?

You would use code similar to this:

EPQ$sex <- factor(EPQ$sex,
  levels = c(0,1),
  labels = c("female", "male"))

Breaking Down Some Code

Baseline <- glm(N_19 ~ Nscore, data = EPQ, family = binomial(link="logit"))

Above is some R studio code for a baseline model that is looking at Item 19 of the Neuroticism Scale on the EPQ. Then below are some questions designed to help you understand each part of the code.

What Does The glm() function do?

This is the function you want to use if you want to run a general linear model.

What Does *N_19 ~ Nscore* mean?

This means that Item 19 is regressed on the overall neuroticism score.

How Would You Modified *N_19 ~ Nscore* To Add In The Sex Variable?

You would simply change *N_19 ~ Nscore* to *N_19 ~ Nscore + Sex*.

How Would You Modify *N_19 ~ Nscore* To Include The Neuroticism and Sex Variable Interaction?

To tell show to run a general linear model on the interaction and that item 19 is regressed onto neuroticism score and sex as part of a Non-Uniformed DIF model, you would change *N_19 ~ Nscore to N_19 ~ Nscore + sex + Nscore:sex*.

What Does *family = binomial(link="logit"))* Mean?

This part of the code is telling R to perform a logistic regression.

In The Output Of An ANOVA for a logistic regression model, what does the deviance column show?

The deviance column shows the chi-square statistic for the model with each subsequent predictor added.

What R Studio Package Is Needed To Obtain *Nagelkerke R Square Effect Sizes?*

You need to use the fmsb package.

What Function Gives You *Nagelkerke R Square Effect Sizes?*

The NalgelkerkeR2() function is the one you need.

Not Really A Question But Here's A Little Pocket Size To Know If DIF Is Present Or Not

Negligible DIF: Chi-square insignificant or Nagelkerke R2 change < 0.035

Moderate DIF: Chi-square significant and Nagelkerke R2 change between 0.035 and 0.07

Large DIF: Chi-square significant and Nagelkerke R2 change ≥ 0.07

How Do You Request exp(B) In R?

So you can interpret them as odds ratios, you simply use the code *exp(coef(Name Of Model))*

MIXED REVISION QUESTIONS

As we head towards the end of the book, I wanted to include a whole bunch of revision questions from a wide range of topics in statistics. You might want to simply read and learn them or you might want to use them in your own revision.

I rather liked looking back over these questions because these questions are similar to the ones that I got wrong on a practice test when I first started revising for my various statistics exams. It was these questions that allowed me to focus on the topics I really needed to practise and whilst I changed the questions slightly, it still allows you to see my personal struggles.

Again, I'm partly open about my own struggles with statistics because I don't want you to judge yourself, criticise yourself and berate yourself for not getting it. Statistics is hard but you can learn it and thrive.

How Is Variance Assigned In Hierarchical Analysis?

In hierarchical analysis, variance shared between multiple independent variables and the dependent variable is assigned to the independent variables that come first causally.

How Many Variables Take Part In A Partial Correlation?

3 variables take part in a partial correlation.

What Is Error Variance?

Error variance is the portion of variance in a datasheet due to extraneous variables and measurement error.

If The Test Scores X Comply With The Classical True-Score Theory, As Well As The Variance Of The Observed Score X Is 10, And The Variance Of Error Is 5, What Is The Variance Of The True Score?

In the True-score model, the True and error variance are additive because the true and error scores are assumed to be uncorrelated.

In other words, $var(Y)=var(T)+var(E)$.

So the right answer is 5.

What Reliability Would You Expect To Have? If You Had A 25-Item Test That Had An Estimated Reliability 0.7. Then You Expanded It To A 100-Item Test By Adding Some Parallel Items.

To calculate the reliability for the 100-item test you would need to use Spearman-Brown formula, which is 4 times longer than the 25-item test with the known reliability of 0.7.

So the right answer to this question would be

0.90

What Type of Data Are Hotel Ratings An Example Of?

Hotel ratings are an example of ordinal data.

What Is The Medium?

The medium is the permissible statistics for ordinal data.

What Does Permissible Refer To In Statistics?

"Permissible" in statistics relates to specific condition as well as criteria.

What Type Of Measurement Are Likert Scales An Example Of?

Likert Scales are an example of measurement by fiat.

What Does Measurement By Fiat Refer To?

Measurement of Fiat refers to methods of quantifying data that isn't meant to be representational. Yet instead it assigns numbers based a intuition, arbitrary units or force validity.

What Is The Aim Of Thurstonian Scaling?

The aim of Thurstonian Scaling is to estimate the means of utilities of ranked stimuli.

What Is Cronbach Alpha Best Suited To?

Cronbach Alpha is best suited to estimate the reliability of a homogenous scale.

What Are Factor Loadings?

Factor loadings are regression coefficients of the observed variables on a factor.

What Are Factor Scores?

Factor scores are estimated scores of a subject on

some latent variable.

What Are Latent Variables?

Latent variables are variables you cannot directly observed nor directly measure.

Why Is A Screen Plot Criterion Helpful?

A scree plot criterion is helpful for determining how many factors to retain since you only retain the factors before and not including the elbow/ elbow point.

In An Exploratory Factor Analysis, Would You Ever Choose An Orthogonal Rotation Over An Oblique One?

In an exploratory factor analysis, there is generally no good reason to choose an orthogonal rotation over an oblique one.

Why Might You Want To Use A Varimax Rotation In A Principal Component Analysis?

You might want to use a principal component analysis with Varimax rotation when you're looking to solve the collinearity problem in a multiple regression.

What's The Main Difference Between A Principal Component Analysis (PCA) And Factor Analysis (FA)?

The main difference between a PCA + FA is in the PCA, the observed variables determine the components, whereas in the factor analysis the common factors cause the observed variables.

What Does Structural Equation Modelling Test?

Structural Equation Modelling tests whether a hypothetical model could have generated the observed data.

What Makes A Structural Equation Modelling Fit Data Well?

For Structural Equation Modelling to fit the data well, the model-implied covariance matrix must not significantly differ from the observed covariance matrix.

What Is Measurement Invariance?

A measure is invariant across your different groups when members of these different groups with the same true score are expected to have the same observed sores. As well as the definition of measurement invariance implies that after we control for the true score, the test score just shouldn't depend on the group that the respondent belongs too.

Also, when it comes to item score, a violation of measurement invariant does constitute as Differential Item Functioning.

What is Configural Invariance?

To have configural invariance, you need to have the same factor model specification holding across the different groups. This means you have to have the same number of factors and loading patterns across the groups.

What Is Metric Invariance?

To have metric invariance, you need equal factor loadings across your different groups to ensure the same scale unit. This allows you to compare the differences between respondents across the groups and you can compare factor variances across the groups as well.

What Is Scalar Invariance?

You have scalar invariance when you have equal intercepts across the different groups because this ensures you have the same scale origin so you can compare respondent's scores and factor means across the different groups.

When Do You Have Uniform Differential Item Functioning In Violations Of Measurement Invariance?

When uniform Differential Item Functioning is present, you'll see that one of your groups has a lower or higher expected item score across all levels of the factor score (True Score). Therefore, this is the main effect of Group on the observed item score.

When Do You Have Non-Uniform Differential Item Functioning In Violations Of Measurement Invariance?

On the other hand, when non-uniform Differential Item Functioning is present, you'll see one of your groups has a higher expected item score in one area of the factor score (again, True Score) distribution, as well as lower expected item score in other areas. Hence, this is the interaction effect of True Score x Group on the observed item score.

What Do You Do When You Have Non-Invariance?

You can adjust for non-invariance in your measurement models by doing a few simple things. You need to release the parameter constraints for non-invariant items so the latent factors will be corrected for the non-invariance and you can use partially invariant models for substantive conclusions and scoring.

What's The Purpose Of Measurement Invariance Studies?

According to Zumbo (2007), we can use measurement invariance studies to try and understand item response processes, investigate the lack of invariance, investigate the comparability of adapted and/ or translated measures, investigate equity and fairness in an assessment and to deal with a possible threat to internal validity. For example, to rule out a measurement artifact as an explanation for the group differences.

Why Are Translated Tests Psychometrically Difficult?

It's common sense to know that we translate different psychometric tests into different languages and adapt them so they can be used in different cultures as well as countries. Yet, there is a very real risk that respondents are unfairly disadvantaged by the translated test because they're not put of the culture the original test was designed for. Since verbal things present us with translation issues, non-verbal items are open to culturally specific interceptions or the respondent might have a disadvantage related to the testing procedure or an additional nuisance factor.

Then even from a theoretical viewpoint, it's very hard to prove that two measurements have a common unit or origin measurement.

What Is Unique Variance Invariance?

You have unique variance invariance when you have equal unique error variances as these ensure the same error of measurement, as well as this precludes systematic sources of error are affecting the score differently across your groups.

What is Statistics Is Used To See If A Structural Equation Model Holds In A Population?

The statistic used to test the hypothesis that a Structural Equation Model holds in the population is chi-square.

What Is The Comparative Fit Index?

Comparative Fit Index is a relative Fit Index so the closer to the CFI is to 1, the better the fit.

How Do You Evaluate Two Structural Equation Models?

To evaluate whether one Structural Equation Model is better than the other, you would run a chi-square difference test to see if the two models are nested.

What Parameters Are Needed To Estimate A Measurement Model?

The factor loadings, covariances of common factors and variances of unique factors are the parameters that need to estimated is a measurement model where the common factors are scaled by setting their variance to 1.

Why Might Two Error Terms Of 2 Observed Variables Be Correlated In Measurement Models?

In measurement models, the error terms of 2 observed variables could be correlated because the 2 items require not only the hypothesised factor, but another construct in common that's unrelated to the factor as well.

What Do Endogenous Variables Have To Have In Path Models?

In path models, every endogenous variable has to have a residual term.

What's The Difference Between A Path Model and Full Structural Equation Model?

The difference between a path model and a full Structural Equation Model is there isn't a measurement part in a path model.

What Is An Endogenous Variable?

An endogenous variable is a dependent variable who's value is determined inside the model and changes in response to changes in other variables.

What Is An Exogenous Variable?

An exogenous variable are independent variables because they aren't affected by other variables in the model. Since their value is determined outside the model.

What's The Difference Between Path Analysis and a Normal Regression Analysis?

The difference between a path analysis and an ordinary regression analysis is a path analysis allows studying several regression models at once.

Why Would You Conduct A Multiple Group Confirmatory Factor Analysis?

You would conduct a multiple group confirmatory factor analysis if you wanted to test whether your model generalises across different populations.

What Does Full Measurement Invariance Assume?

Full Measurement (Strict Factorial Invariance) in repeated measures assumes that there are equal intercepts, factor loadings and unique variances across measurement occasion.

What Is Differential Item Functioning?

Differential Item Functioning (DIF) is observed when examinees from different groups have different probabilities of responding correctly to or endorsing an item after matching the ability on the ability that the item measures.

What Is The Aim Of Judgement Scaling?

The aim of judgement scaling is to scale item scores based on empirical evidence.

When Would A 5-Point Scale Be Classed as Difficult?

Your item would be classed as difficult if you had a 5-point frequency scale running from "Never" to "Always" and 90% of your respondents put "Never".

Does Cronbach's Alpha Require All Items To Have The Same Difficulty?

No, Cronbach's Alpha doesn't require all items to have the same difficulties.

What Would Influence The Reliability Of Two Parrel Forms Of A Test being Administered In The Same Test Session?

When two parrel forms of a test are administered in the same test session, their reliability measurements aren't influenced by memory effects. Yet they are influenced by measurement precision of either form and participant fatigue.

ITEM RESPONSE THEORY

To wrap up this book in terms of questions, I have to admit that I do enjoy learning about Item Response Theory, because it makes you think about items, questions and the tests that we use in psychology. As well as whilst this is a separate topic from Structural Equation Modelling, it is a logical next step and if you really allow yourself to get immersed in the topic then this can almost be fun.

<u>What Is Item Response Theory?</u>

Whilst this is a statistical theory, I don't really like the term because this isn't a theory like other ones in psychology where you can just explain it. Instead at this point in the chapter all I can say is Item Response Theory is a paradigm within psychometrics that deals with the questionnaires, scoring of tests, analysis and design as well as similar instruments that aim to measure attitudes, abilities and other variables.

What Is The Aim Of Item Response Theory?

Item Response Theory aims to explain the relationship between latent traits and observed responses or outcomes.

What Are The Only Two Assumptions We make When Modelling Categorical Item Responses?

The first assumption is that the responses to the item are independent after we control for the latent trait. This is exactly the same as our assumption in factor analysis where we called it "local independence" since if no common variance is left in the items after accounting for the latent trait then there is only one dimension. That is the trait or factor that underlies the item responses.

Secondly, we assume the shape of a function linking the item response and the factor is logistic.

What Is Item Discrimination In Item Response Theory?

Item discrimination refers to the rate of how the probability of endorsing a correct item changes given a respondent's ability level. If it's high then the item effectively discriminates between individuals at different trait levels. Whereas if it's low then the item doesn't differentiate well and it might not be sensitive to variations in the latent trait.

What Is Item Difficulty In Item Response Theory?

Item Difficulty is the parameter referring to the level of ability needed for respondents to have a 50% chance of endorsing the correct item.

What Are Item Characteristic Curves?

These curves are the probability of the correct responses that are conditional on the latent "ability" or any other trait that you're interested in. Also, these curves are bound between 0 and 1, as well as the probability increases monotonically (so it never decreases) as the respondent's ability increases.

In Item Response Theory, How Is The Item Response Regressed?

When it comes to Item Response Theory, the item response is regressed onto the latent trait. Therefore, the higher the Item Difficulty value, the more difficult the item is to pass.

What is The Rasch Model?

Rasch (1960) proposed a model made up of a simple relationship between an item's difficulty and a respondent's ability and you can use this to describe the odds of someone passing the item. The equation is log odds($u_i=1$) = **ability** − **difficulty**$_i$ and it's interesting to note that when ability and difficulty are the same the odds of a respondent passing the item is 50% or 0.5.

In addition, when the Rasch Model holds the items are ordered in the same way regardless of the sample used to test the model, and the same ordering of people is obtained regardless of the item combination used. As well as the number of items passed is a sufficient statistic for measuring someone's ability.

Overall, that's why when you look at Item

Characteristic Curves, it is only the item difficulties that vary, and the lines don't cross.

What Are 1-Parameter Logistic Models?

These models use the Rasch Model with a latent trait that's scaled like a z-score so mathematically it looks like this, log odds(u_i=1) = **discrimination(ability – difficulty$_i$)** and B_1 = discrimination and scaling coefficient.

In this model the items might vary in difficulty but the discrimination parameters are equal across the different items. Therefore, ability is the person parameter and difficulty is the item parameter. Also, both the person and items are on the same scale.

What Are 2-Paramter Logistic Models?

Whereas these models focus on the probability of the respondent giving the correct response and this is dependent on the person's ability (that we scale like a z-score) and two item parameters. For instance, log odds(u_i=1) = **discrimination$_i$(ability – difficulty$_i$)**.

Interestingly, the first-ever Item Response Theory model was a 2-parameter model by Lord (1952) where he used a different link function. This isn't a logit function but a normal probit or ogive function. Then Birnbaum suggested Lord should use the logistic function for simplicity of calculation in the 1950s.

What Are 3-Parameter Logistic Models?

Personally, I think these are some of the more important models in statistics because this type of model accounts for guessing.

This was introduced by Birnbaum (1968) because the researcher wanted to add in a parameter to account for guessing. Like log odds($u_i=1$) = **guessing$_i$** + (1 − **guessing$_i$**)[**discrimination$_i$(ability − difficulty$_i$)**].

In other words, when we take guessing into account on something like a multiple-choice test, the guessing parameter is typically close to 1/ K. K is the number of the alternatives.

What Is Maximum Likelihood Estimation?

This method finds a score that maximises the likelihood of the observed response so there aren't any finite scores for a "perfect" response pattern, and convergence isn't guaranteed with aberrant responses. Also, prior information on score distribution, like Bayesian estimation, can be added too.

What Is Standard Error of Measurement In Item Response Theory?

This is the likelihood of a response pattern having a distribution because a lot of scores are possible but not all of them are equally likely to occur. Therefore, we can look at the likelihood distribution for three different response patterns and this is where the Standard Deviation of the Likelihood comes in. Since this is where the standard error of the estimated score comes from, and it is the Standard Error that depends on the response pattern.

What Is The Difference Between Test Characteristic Curves And Item Characteristic Curves?

Unlike Item Characteristic Curves that plot the expected item score of a given latent trait, a Test Characteristic Curve is the sum of all the expected test scores (true scores) on the given latent trait.

Item Response Theory R Studio Questions
What Does The ltm Package Stand For?

This package stands for Latent Trait Modelling and you need it for item response theory modelling.

What Function Do You Use To Fit A Rasch Model?

In R Studio, you need to use the rasch() function. Then you can see the results by using the summary() function. Your R code will look something like this *fit1PL <- rasch(your_data)*.

How Do You Fit A 2-parameter Model In R Studio?

You use the ltm() function and your code will look something like this *fit2PL <- ltm(your_data~z1)*.

How Do You Get Your Model Coefficients In A Convenient Format?

You need to use the coef() function in the ltm package. For example, *coef(fti2PL)*.

How Do You Get Item Characteristic Curves In R Studio?

You can get the Item Characteristic Curves by plotting the items using the plot() function.

How Do You Compare A 1-Parameter and 2-Parameter Model In R Studio?

After creating your two models, you can compare them using the R Base function anova() and this will allow you to see which model fits better.

What Do You Need To Careful About When Using The factor.scores() function In R?

You need to be careful about the psych package since this package has a factor.scores() function just like the ltm package. If you have both activated then R Studio might make an error and run the factor.scores() function from the psych package instead of ltm. This means you should either make sure your psych package isn't activated or specify to R you want the function from the ltm package. You can do this by putting the name of the package in front of the function, like *ltm::factor.scores()*.

CONCLUSION

I have to admit that I am extremely happy that I wrote this book for myself and you wonderful readers. Since this book actually formed a core part of my own revision for my Spring Term exams in my Masters.

I found writing this book really useful because it forced me to focus on every topic, each definition and each concept in a lot more depth than I normally would have. I needed to think about what sort of questions and information would be useful for you and I needed to make sure I understood it myself too.

That's the first thing I want to thank you for, because without wonderful readers like you, I wouldn't be able to do fun projects like this book. I wouldn't have the motivation or even an idea about how to elevate my revision game to the level that I needed for these statistic exams.

So thank you.

Secondly, for a long time, I have been wanting to

do something on statistics to help psychology students, because I know it is a massive area of anxiety and fear. I don't blame them because there have been a lot of times on my psychology journey where I have felt the same fear.

Therefore, I'm glad that I was able to finally do something to help psychology students and I truly hope that you feel like you have a better understanding of psychology statistics now.

Of course, this book was never meant to be a replacement for a lecturer and a textbook, but I hope it helped. I know it helped me and thinking about statistics in terms of questions really did help my understanding for my own exams.

Overall, whether you're an undergraduate or postgraduate psychology student, I wish you the best of luck on your psychology journey. And I hope you now feel better able to not only survive statistics, but thrive.

https://www.subscribepage.io/psychologyboxset

CHECK OUT THE PSYCHOLOGY WORLD PODCAST FOR MORE PSYCHOLOGY INFORMATION! AVAILABLE ON ALL MAJOR PODCAST APPS.

About the author:

Connor Whiteley is the author of over 60 books in the sci-fi fantasy, nonfiction psychology and books for writer's genre and he is a Human Branding Speaker and Consultant.

He is a passionate warhammer 40,000 reader, psychology student and author.

Who narrates his own audiobooks and he hosts The Psychology World Podcast.

All whilst studying Psychology at the University of Kent, England.

Also, he was a former Explorer Scout where he gave a speech to the Maltese President in August 2018 and he attended Prince Charles' 70th Birthday Party at Buckingham Palace in May 2018.

Plus, he is a self-confessed coffee lover!

CONNOR WHITELEY

All books in 'An Introductory Series':
Clinical Psychology and Transgender Clients
Clinical Psychology
Moral Psychology
Myths About Clinical Psychology
401 Statistics Questions For Psychology Students
Careers In Psychology
Psychology of Suicide
Dementia Psychology
Clinical Psychology Reflections Volume 4
Forensic Psychology of Terrorism And Hostage-Taking
Forensic Psychology of False Allegations
Year In Psychology
CBT For Anxiety
CBT For Depression
Applied Psychology
BIOLOGICAL PSYCHOLOGY 3RD EDITION
COGNITIVE PSYCHOLOGY THIRD EDITION
SOCIAL PSYCHOLOGY- 3RD EDITION
ABNORMAL PSYCHOLOGY 3RD EDITION
PSYCHOLOGY OF RELATIONSHIPS- 3RD EDITION

401 STATISTICS QUESTIONS FOR PSYCHOLOGY STUDENTS

DEVELOPMENTAL PSYCHOLOGY 3RD EDITION
HEALTH PSYCHOLOGY
RESEARCH IN PSYCHOLOGY
A GUIDE TO MENTAL HEALTH AND TREATMENT AROUND THE WORLD- A GLOBAL LOOK AT DEPRESSION
FORENSIC PSYCHOLOGY
THE FORENSIC PSYCHOLOGY OF THEFT, BURGLARY AND OTHER CRIMES AGAINST PROPERTY
CRIMINAL PROFILING: A FORENSIC PSYCHOLOGY GUIDE TO FBI PROFILING AND GEOGRAPHICAL AND STATISTICAL PROFILING.
CLINICAL PSYCHOLOGY FORMULATION IN PSYCHOTHERAPY
PERSONALITY PSYCHOLOGY AND INDIVIDUAL DIFFERENCES
CLINICAL PSYCHOLOGY REFLECTIONS VOLUME 1
CLINICAL PSYCHOLOGY REFLECTIONS VOLUME 2
Clinical Psychology Reflections Volume 3
CULT PSYCHOLOGY
Police Psychology

A Psychology Student's Guide To University
How Does University Work?
A Student's Guide To University And Learning
University Mental Health and Mindset

Other books by Connor Whiteley:
Bettie English Private Eye Series
A Very Private Woman
The Russian Case
A Very Urgent Matter
A Case Most Personal
Trains, Scots and Private Eyes
The Federation Protects
Cops, Robbers and Private Eyes
Just Ask Bettie English
An Inheritance To Die For
The Death of Graham Adams
Bearing Witness
The Twelve
The Wrong Body
The Assassination Of Bettie English
Wining And Dying
Eight Hours
Uniformed Cabal
A Case Most Christmas

401 STATISTICS QUESTIONS FOR PSYCHOLOGY STUDENTS

<u>Gay Romance Novellas</u>
Breaking, Nursing, Repairing A Broken Heart
Jacob And Daniel
Fallen For A Lie
Spying And Weddings
Clean Break
Awakening Love
Meeting A Country Man
Loving Prime Minister
Snowed In Love
Never Been Kissed
Love Betrays You

<u>Lord of War Origin Trilogy:</u>
Not Scared Of The Dark
Madness
Burn Them All

<u>Way Of The Odyssey</u>
Odyssey of Rebirth
Convergence of Odysseys

<u>Lady Tano Fantasy Adventure Stories</u>
Betrayal
Murder
Annihilation

The Fireheart Fantasy Series
Heart of Fire
Heart of Lies
Heart of Prophecy
Heart of Bones
Heart of Fate

City of Assassins (Urban Fantasy)
City of Death
City of Martyrs
City of Pleasure
City of Power

Agents of The Emperor
Return of The Ancient Ones
Vigilance
Angels of Fire
Kingmaker
The Eight
The Lost Generation
Hunt
Emperor's Council
Speaker of Treachery
Birth Of The Empire
Terraforma
Spaceguard

401 STATISTICS QUESTIONS FOR PSYCHOLOGY STUDENTS

<u>The Rising Augusta Fantasy Adventure Series</u>
Rise To Power
Rising Walls
Rising Force
Rising Realm

<u>Lord Of War Trilogy (Agents of The Emperor)</u>
Not Scared Of The Dark
Madness
Burn It All Down

<u>Miscellaneous:</u>
RETURN
FREEDOM
SALVATION
Reflection of Mount Flame
The Masked One
The Great Deer
English Independence

OTHER SHORT STORIES BY CONNOR WHITELEY

<u>Mystery Short Story Collections</u>
Criminally Good Stories Volume 1: 20 Detective Mystery Short Stories
Criminally Good Stories Volume 2: 20 Private

Investigator Short Stories
Criminally Good Stories Volume 3: 20 Crime Fiction Short Stories
Criminally Good Stories Volume 4: 20 Science Fiction and Fantasy Mystery Short Stories
Criminally Good Stories Volume 5: 20 Romantic Suspense Short Stories

Connor Whiteley Starter Collections:
Agents of The Emperor Starter Collection
Bettie English Starter Collection
Matilda Plum Starter Collection
Gay Romance Starter Collection
Way Of The Odyssey Starter Collection
Kendra Detective Fiction Starter Collection

Mystery Short Stories:
Protecting The Woman She Hated
Finding A Royal Friend
Our Woman In Paris
Corrupt Driving
A Prime Assassination
Jubilee Thief
Jubilee, Terror, Celebrations
Negative Jubilation
Ghostly Jubilation

401 STATISTICS QUESTIONS FOR PSYCHOLOGY STUDENTS

Killing For Womenkind
A Snowy Death
Miracle Of Death
A Spy In Rome
The 12:30 To St Pancreas
A Country In Trouble
A Smokey Way To Go
A Spicy Way To GO
A Marketing Way To Go
A Missing Way To Go
A Showering Way To Go
Poison In The Candy Cane
Kendra Detective Mystery Collection Volume 1
Kendra Detective Mystery Collection Volume 2
Mystery Short Story Collection Volume 1
Mystery Short Story Collection Volume 2
Criminal Performance
Candy Detectives
Key To Birth In The Past

<u>Science Fiction Short Stories:</u>
Their Brave New World
Gummy Bear Detective
The Candy Detective
What Candies Fear

The Blurred Image
Shattered Legions
The First Rememberer
Life of A Rememberer
System of Wonder
Lifesaver
Remarkable Way She Died
The Interrogation of Annabella Stormic
Blade of The Emperor
Arbiter's Truth
Computation of Battle
Old One's Wrath
Puppets and Masters
Ship of Plague
Interrogation
Edge of Failure

Fantasy Short Stories:
City of Snow
City of Light
City of Vengeance
Dragons, Goats and Kingdom
Smog The Pathetic Dragon
Don't Go In The Shed
The Tomato Saver
The Remarkable Way She Died
Dragon Coins